HOW LONG?

How Long?

PRISON REFLECTIONS FROM THE PHILIPPINES

by Karl Gaspar

Edited by
HELEN GRAHAM, M.M.,
and
BREDA NOONAN, S.S.C.

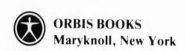

ORBIS BOOKS
Maryknoll, New York

BIP-90

DOVE COMMUNICATIONS
Melbourne, Australia

The Catholic Foreign Mission Society of America (Maryknoll) recruits and trains people for overseas missionary service. Through Orbis Books Maryknoll aims to foster the international dialogue that is essential to mission. The books published, however, reflect the opinions of their authors and are not meant to represent the official position of the society.

Original edition copyright © 1984 by Claretian Publications, U.P. P.O. Box 4, Quezon City 3004, Philippines
United States edition published in 1986 by Orbis Books, Maryknoll, NY 10545
Manufactured in the United States of America

Manuscript editor: William H. Schlau

Library of Congress Cataloging-in-Publication Data
Gaspar, Karl, 1947-
  How long?

  1. Gaspar, Karl, 1947-   . 2. Prisoners—
Philippines. 3. Persecution—Philippines.
4. Philippines—Politics and government—1973-
5. Meditations. I. Graham, Helen. II. Noonan, Breda.
III. Title.
BX4705.G2566A34 1986   282′.092′4 [B]   85-25851
ISBN 0-88344-226-4 (pbk.)

Published in Australia in 1986 by Dove Communications, Box 316 Blackburn, Victoria 3130

Dove ISBN 0-85924-444-X

To

Edgar, Amy, Betty, Dong,
Nat, Edwin, Oca, Jo,
Tony, Charlie, Eva, Jun,

and the other political detainees
who spent time
at the Davao City Detention Center
in 1983–84

for helping me survive
the long wait for freedom

Contents

Foreword

I met Karl Gaspar in January, 1983. We were both in Geneva for a dialogue between First and Third World theologians.

Conferences, I must admit, are not my favorite things. The best part about them, and often the redeeming aspect, is the people you meet. And sometimes, if you are fortunate, a new friendship is made which makes the whole trip worthwhile.

During that week, Karl Gaspar and I became friends. The sense of kindred spirit and common struggles came easily and quickly. We are the same age. Both of us have come out of the student movements of the 1960s, he in the Philippines, and now root our activism in a deeply held Christian commitment. We each do theology for the sake of building a grassroots movement in the churches, and both work closely with small "base communities" emerging throughout the church in our two countries.

During the busy conference schedule we found time to take long walks and to talk about the gospel and what it means for us. We spoke of our backgrounds, families, theological work, political struggles, and personal lives.

The sometimes academic and overly rhetorical nature of the conference bothered us both. I laughed and then almost cried when Karl carried out his assignment to report from our small group to the plenary session by improvising a drama and dance to convey what we had discussed. His spontaneity and creativity were infectious as Karl brought genuine feeling and joy to the often dry proceedings of the conference.

Karl is indeed a charismatic figure and has a sense of humor that is too rare among those who daily struggle for justice and peace. For our closing worship celebration Karl painted a banner which captured the spirit and struggles represented by the conference participants better than all the speeches that had been made.

vii

I enjoyed and respected the many facets of my new friend— church worker, activist, artist, musician, dancer, pastor, brother. When we said good-bye, I could feel the personal bond that had been formed. Then we both returned home to our busy lives.

In March I received a letter from Karl. In it he spoke of the friendship between us, saying, "It will take a miracle to get us together again, but the bond between us will remain strong."

Three days later, I got a phone call—Karl had disappeared. Eyewitnesses reported that he had been picked up by the military the day before Palm Sunday.

The days that followed were filled with the efforts of Karl's many friends to draw international attention to his disappearance, for the sake of discovering his whereabouts, protecting his safety, and defending his life. Phone calls and cables were filed with the State Department by sympathetic members of Congress. The press was alerted.

We did everything we could think of to do. We knew Karl's life was at stake. I even resorted to calling Philippine President Marcos's palace and the Ministry of Defense to register my concern for Karl. They seemed taken aback by an American pastor calling from that distance and being so insistent. "And what is *your* name?" they wanted to know.

Preoccupation with Karl's well-being became my reflection for Holy Week. Where had they taken him, what had they done to him, is he being tortured, is he still alive? I thought of the painful questions of Holy Week for Karl's family and friends. My prayers for Karl were desperate and intense; I felt helpless.

I fasted through the weekend and later learned that Karl had been fasting too. He was on a hunger strike to protest his illegal detention and the denial of his constitutional rights.

On Easter Sunday, our community had a sunrise service. I did the homily and Eucharist. There was still no news of Karl. As the sun came up, however, I knew that if Karl were still alive, he would be celebrating Easter too. For the first time, I had a deep sense that Karl's faith and God's grace would bring him through.

A few days later, Karl's whereabouts were made known, no doubt in response to all the attention. He had been moved to a detention camp in Manila and was being held on some trumped-up charges of inciting rebellion or the like.

Then I received a letter from Karl. In it he shared the following reflections:

"On March 23, I got a copy of the March (Nicaragua) issue of *Sojourners*. By March 25 before I went to sleep, I had read it cover to cover. . . . One of the things that really struck me was a quote in the interview of Fr. Miguel [D'Escoto] where he said: 'We should always be ready to embrace our cross. . . .'

"March 26 I was to be confronted with my challenge to embrace my own cross. I was arrested by the military. For close to two weeks I was confined in a 'safehouse' and later put in solitary confinement in a small room in a military camp here in Manila. . . . In our situation, one is guilty until proven innocent. Thus, I will be detained until God knows when.

"But don't worry. I'm okay and in fact I feel privileged with this 'gift' of detention. It was very significant that all this happened during Holy Week. I was thus able to enter into Christ's own experience of pain, anguish, agony, despair, suffering, resignation, and hope. And with His grace I was able to embrace my cross fully and survived. . . . What really was the thread that kept my reflections intact was the image provided by Fr. Miguel, through *Sojourners*.

"I thought of you and prayed for you during my detention as I prayed for all friends. I remembered our long talk at the tower of the old cathedral in the old section of Geneva. . . . Your kind words helped keep me strong during my long vigil.

"I prayed that you and the members of your community grow in strength and courage to face more crucial tests. . . . Maybe one day you can come to the Philippines so we can also have a special issue on the Philippines."

It was almost two years later when the long-awaited news finally came.

Karl Gaspar is free!

For one who loves freedom and beauty as much as Karl, captivity is a painful and difficult thing. And yet, the imprisonment of Karl Gaspar was absolutely full of the grace of God.

His letters read like modern-day prison epistles. They chronicle the honest human struggles, the persistent faith, and the unquenchable hope of a brother who has put his life in God's hands. In mysterious and miraculous ways, the testimony of Karl's imprisonment has served to build faith, strengthen conviction, quicken conscience, and "equip the saints," in more places and ways than Karl could ever imagine.

The Marcos regime put Karl in prison to silence him and put an end to his activities on behalf of justice and freedom. Instead, his voice became even more strong and clear and was heard around the world. And the cause to which he has given his life has been greatly served by Karl's prison sojourn.

When I heard that Karl had been acquitted, I ran all around the office excitedly telling everyone the good news. When I heard that he had been released, I felt my heart leap for joy.

My then-9-year-old nephew, Nathan, had written Karl a letter. Karl was in the process of writing him back when he was released. So, Nathan was one of the first to hear the story of what Karl did when he got out of jail. Karl wrote Nathan, "Before I could mail this letter I got released. Finally, after a long wait, the Supreme Court ordered the military to release me this afternoon. I feel great, and we celebrated with ice cream and a swim at the beach. Praise the Lord!"

Karl's particular sensitivity to his fellow prisoners was evident thoughout his letters. I know he will not be satisfied until all the captives have been set free. But we rejoice that one captive has been set free. We rejoice that in his captivity and in his freedom the purposes and love of God have been made known throughout the earth. May God be praised. We love you, Karl, and our hearts are filled with thanksgiving.

JIM WALLIS

Editors' Preface

On March 26, 1983, Karl Gaspar disappeared. After two weeks of persistent denial of any knowledge of his whereabouts, the military finally announced it had arrested him. Karl's disappearance evoked national and international concern: letters, telephone calls, and cables poured in from all over the world. Such widespread concern highlighted the extensive influence of this Filipino national. Who is Karl and why this concern?

One article written after his arrest described Karl as "a lay theologian and church worker, a poet, artist, dramatist, musician, and long-term human rights activist." But, for many, Karl's impact lies in his total commitment of himself and his gifts to the Filipino people in their struggle for personal and national liberation. This commitment to work for and speak on behalf of the people and their struggle brought him to many countries through the sponsorship of different church organizations. Wherever he went he made friends, friends who did not forget him or the people whose lives and struggle he shared. His friends understood his disappearance on March 26 could have occurred only as a consequence of that commitment.

As soon as the military allowed contact between Karl and his family, he began to write and share his reflections on events as they unfolded. Thus began the phenomenal correspondence Karl has maintained since that eventful day in March. Some of the letters and reflections have already been circulated, but it was felt that a more comprehensive publication would enable the message of this political detainee to reach even more people.

The editing of this material has been a welcome task; Karl is a close personal friend and a person whose commitment has had a deep influence on us. Through his correspondence he overcame the effort to silence him and render him ineffective in his witness to the promise of socially transformed Philippines. We are glad to play even a small role in helping him work to fulfill this challenge. Material included in this publication covers the period from his arrest in March 1983 until his trial in Davao City in August 1984. We are very grateful to all who, so readily, made available personal letters and other materials, and who graciously gave their time to type or proofread the manuscript.

The challenge of these reflections is not confined to those who oppressively wield power. They are also a challenge to us who claim to share Karl's faith and commitment to a Philippines and a world socially transformed. Herein lies the deeper significance of his writings. They are not just about Karl; Karl is not the focus. His story, as he reflects upon it and its meaning, becomes a story within a story, a drama within a drama. The wider story, the focus, is the imprisonment of the Philippines today. Bishop Escaler said at Karl's trial that his imprisonment was diabolical. The imprisonment of the country is no less.

The story of the Philippines is becoming more and more a story of lies, guns, torture, prisons, and death. The political detainees embody this grim reality. Their commitment to justice, freedom, and true peace for their people has led to their imprisonment. Imprisonment is a questionable means of punishment when used by any government, but when used by governments to remove thousands of men and women committed to social change it is a sign of deep fear. The fear is of the dream and vision these men and women hold in their hearts. Karl exposes this fear for what it is and witnesses to the world that no prison wall can contain the dream, let alone destroy it.

As Karl shares his own pain and journey he symbolizes the pain and journey of his people in their struggle. But, above all, in his hope and in his song he symbolizes the indomitable spirit of his people. Just as his spirit seems to grow stronger and stronger as the months pass in prison, so the spirit of the people is becoming more alive and more militant as efforts to kill their dream become more brutal. No matter what happens they will not allow the dream to die. They know that some day it will be realized. But . . . HOW LONG?

HELEN GRAHAM, M.M. AND BREDA NOONAN, S.S.C.

Preface

> . . . But what else is there to do when you are alone for days in the dull monotony of a narrow cell other than write long letters, think strange thoughts, and pray long prayers.
> *Martin Luther King from a jail in Birmingham*

After I was surfaced [April 9, 1983] by the military I started writing long letters to friends, and, as a response, my own mail became quite voluminous. Even with all the time on hand in prison it became impossible to personally answer all these letters, and it also became boring to repeat the same information and thoughts. So "Letters to Friends" was born.

During these past, long months of my detention I must have written hundreds of letters, a few articles, and poems. While I am still here, I may continue the writing. At first I had doubts about publishing the letters, but friends convinced me of the possible value of the book. I am glad that Helen and Breda have seriously pursued this project, and I am certainly indebted to their valuable editing. I am grateful to the Columban Fathers for financially assisting their work.

I am also grateful to Fred and Helen and the rest of my family for their encouragement and inspiration. Their availability and ready service made the endeavor of writing possible.

Finally, to all of you, my friends, to whom these letters have been addressed, thank you. Your friendship has helped me survive the days of wrath and the nights of despair; your letters have provoked these responses; and your encouragement has made possible these simple reflections.

KARL GASPAR
AUGUST 17, 1984

Biographical Chronology

1947   Carlito (Karl) Gaspar born June 8 in Davao City.
                Karl is the third of eight children born to Salvador
                Gaspar and Josefina Morante.

1967   Received an A.B. in social sciences from the Ate-
                neo de Davao University, Davao City.

1967–68   Writer for the Society of the Divine Word's
                (S.V.D.) *Mission World* magazine (Manila).

1968–71   Research associate in ASI's research department.

1970   Received an M.S. in economics from the Asian
                Social Institute (ASI), Manila.

1971–72   College teacher at HCCD, Digos, Davao del Sur.
                He set up a socioeconomic society which had a
                students' theatre group called *Mga Magtutulang
                Mayukmok* (the theatre of small folks) which
                specialized in conscientization plays.

1972–74   Member of the parish team headed by the Mary-
                knoll Fathers in Mati, Davao Oriental. Karl and
                his two companions were arrested when martial
                law was declared (Sept. 23, 1972). The three were
                detained overnight and were under house arrest
                for three months.

1974–76   Member of the Philippine Business for Social
                Progress (PBSP) Mindanao team based in Davao

City, first as a research officer and later on as regional manager for Mindanao.

He set up *Alay Kapwa* (offering to the neighbor) theater group composed of students and young professionals from Davao City and was also instrumental in the establishment of the Citizens' Council for Justice and Peace, the ecumenical forerunner of the CCJPs in Mindanao.

1976–77   Invited, along with four other Filipino churchworkers, to Ireland by TROCAIRE to give talks and engage in dialogue on church and development issues. At this time, Karl traveled through Europe, North America, and Japan to meet justice and peace groups, to give talks on justice and development issues, and to meet with representatives of various development agencies.

1977–80   Elected executive secretary of the Mindanao-Sulu Pastoral Conference Secretariat (MSPCS).

1979   Delegate to the Asian Theological Conference (ATC) held in Sri Lanka and sponsored by the Ecumenical Association of Third World Theologians (EATWOT).

1980   Represented the Philippines at CEBEMO's tenth anniversary celebration in Holland; gave talks in the U.S. and Canada; engaged in a study tour in Central and South America on the church's basic Christian communities (BCCs), justice and peace activities, and theological concerns.

1981   Gave talks in Australia in February at the invitation of the Columban Fathers' Justice and Peace Office. From May to August, Karl gave talks in the U.S. at the invitation of the Maryknoll Fathers' Justice and Peace Office.

1982   Assisted the Office of Human Development
                (OHD) in preparing exposure programs for
                APHD in Sri Lanka and also the exposure pro-
                gram of the Action for World Development
                (AWD) in the Philippines.

1982   Development education officer for NASSA (Na-
                tional Secretariat of Social Action of the Catholic
                Bishops Conference of the Philippines); in Febru-
                ary Karl gave talks in Australia for the Catholic
                Committee for Justice and Peace.

1983   Attended the Ecumenical Association of Third
                World Theologians (EATWOT) convention in
                Geneva (Jan.–Feb.) and became an EATWOT
                member. On the way home Karl attended a con-
                ference on popular theatre in Bangladesh. In
                March he began his work as executive secretary of
                the Resources Development Foundation of the
                Philippines (RDFP).

1983   *March 26:* Karl left his office at the RDFP just
                before 5:00 P.M. to pay a farewell visit to Volker
                Schmidt, a German pastor who was scheduled to
                leave in a few days for Germany. He did not
                return home that evening or the next day. The
                local Sunday paper carried the headline that
                Volker and four others had been arrested several
                days earlier. Karl's family began to suspect that
                Karl may have been picked up by the military at
                Volker's house. The suspicion was confirmed the
                next day when Volker was able to reveal that the
                military had asked him if he knew "a certain Karl
                Gaspar." Repeatedly the family, lawyers, the
                archbishop of Davao, and friends received a neg-
                ative answer when they questioned the military as
                to whether or not it had Karl in its custody. Family
                and friends checked hospitals and funeral par-
                lors. But Karl was nowhere to be found.

March 29: A petition for the writ of *habeas corpus* (dated March 28) was filed with the supreme court by Helen Gaspar through her counsel, Atty. José W. Diokno. An amended petition was filed on April 4 after a news item (*Bulletin Today,* April 3, 1983) admitted that Karl was in military custody and indicated that a PCO had been subsequently issued by the president on March 29.

Karl was flown by military airplane from Davao, Mindanao, to Nichols Air Base in Metro Manila; during his transfer he was blindfolded, had masking tape and dark glasses over his eyes, cotton plugs in his ears, a bag on his head, and was handcuffed and dressed in an air force fatigue uniform placed over his civilian clothes. From Nichols Air Base he was taken to the 15th MIG compound at Bago Bantay, Quezon City, where he was detained until May 6.

April 9: Easter Sunday. Karl's sister Beatrize was able to visit him in Camp Bago Bantay. His first "Dear Friends" letter was sent out through his sister.

April 10: Thinking that he was going to see the minister of national defense, Juan Ponce Enrile, Karl was tricked into a press conference. Karl took exception to the news releases which followed and wrote to the two major government-controlled dailies (letters dated April 15).

April 14: A supreme court hearing was held in Manila on the petitions for the writ of *habeas corpus* filed by members of Karl's family.

May 10: Karl was transferred from Camp Bago Bantay in Manila to the Metropolitan District Command (MetroDisCom) Detention Center on the compound in the Philippine Constabulary (PC) in Davao City, Mindanao.

May 19: A case of "conspiracy to commit rebellion" was filed against Karl with the Davao

City fiscal. Previously on April 6, the military had filed a case of "conspiracy to commit rebellion" and, two days later, added the charge of "illegal possession of ammunition." The Davao City fiscal's office ruled on May 4 that there was a *prima facie* case only for the first charge, and the case for inciting to rebellion was filed.

June 12: Close to sixty detainees began a fast on the occasion of the celebration of Philippine independence. The fast was to last for thirty-three days. On July 14 the members of the group decided to declare a full hunger strike because there was no response from the military regarding their demands. Among the ten demands listed in the group's statement were the following: (1) abolish the PCO and restore the democratic and constitutional rights of all prisoners; (2) stop the "salvaging" of prisoners; (3) stop all illegal transfer of prisoners for purposes of torture, interrogation, or guidance of military operations; (4) release all prisoners who (*a*) have not been formally charged, (*b*) are less than eighteen years of age, or (*c*) have serious physical and/or mental disorders.

July 20: Karl and Volker, who were the suspected leaders of the hunger strike, were transferred from the detention center to the city jail in Ma-a, some seven kilometers outside the center of town.

July 25: Karl and Volker began eating after it was communicated to them that the others (at the detention center) had agreed to stop the hunger strike in return for Col. Valderama's promise to grant the majority of their demands.

1984   *May 22:* A motion to quash the charges against him was filed by Karl's lawyers on the basis of lack of evidence against Karl.

August 15, 16, and 17: The motion to quash

having been denied (July 7), marathon hearings were scheduled for the defense to prove that there was a lack of evidence in the case. The hearings were held August 15–17 in Davao City. Among the witnesses in Karl's behalf were bishops Federico O. Escaler, S.J., and Bienvenido S. Tudtud.

1985   *January 31:* Five months after the end of Karl's trial and more than two months beyond the legal time allowed, Judge Bernardo Saludares summoned Karl to a court hearing in Davao city. There he declared that "the accused Carlito Gaspar be acquitted of the charge and ordered immediately discharged from the custody of the law." But a declaration of innocence is no guarantee of freedom in the Philippines today as a detainee with a PCO can be released from custody of the military only by the president himself. After the hearing Karl returned to the stockade.

February 6: Atty. José Diokno filed an urgent motion to the supreme court for the immediate release of Karl.

February 7: The supreme court issued a resolution ordering the immediate release.

February 9: Gen. Fidel Ramos, acting chief of staff of the armed forces, was in Davao City. On being informed of the decision of the supreme court, he ordered the immediate "temporary" release of Karl and it became effective at 3:00 P.M. Friends gathered and a thanksgiving mass was celebrated.

Karl is free, at least "temporarily," but more than one thousand political detainees remain in detention throughout the country.

A Personal Word

I consider it a rare privilege to have been requested by the editors of this book to write a few words about the author and his letters. Since 1962—I was then president and rector of the Ateneo de Davao—our paths have frequently crossed. For three years (1977 to 1980) when he held the position of executive secretary of the Mindanao-Sulu Pastoral Conference, we worked together striving to extend the services of the MSPC to all the twenty dioceses and prelatures in Mindanao-Sulu. We also shared the speakers' platform on many occasions. From these experiences I have learned to appreciate the personality of Karl as a true and sincere Christian, a real patriot, and a prophet with a message to all peoples struggling to live their lives as responsible Christian citizens in the midst of a systematic and structured suppression of human rights.

Karl Gaspar's letters from his prison cell reflect the varying moods of the persecuted and detained. The first moods seemed like cries of abandonment and rage; then gradually hope emerged and a deep conviction that the sufferings of the detained could in God's wisdom serve a purpose of awakening fearful consciences toward the realization that if this could happen to one person, it could also happen to all of us.

It is my hope, therefore, that as readers go through the letters of Karl Gaspar, they may appreciate the Christian faith more sincerely and live it more fully whether in joy or in pain.

FEDERICO O. ESCALER, S.J.
BISHOP OF IPIL

1

The Beginning

Dear Jim,[*]

On March 23, I got a copy of the March [Nicaragua] issue of *Sojourners*. . . . One of the things that really struck me was a quote in the interview of Fr. Miguel [D'Escoto] where he said: "We should always be ready to embrace our cross. . . ."

Karl

MARCH 26: AN UNFORGETTABLE SOJOURN

It was 4:35 in the afternoon of Saturday, March 26, 1983. Karl had left work early to call on Pastor Volker Schmidt, who was due to leave Davao the next day. Unknown to him Volker's apartment had been raided, and the pastor and three companions had been arrested.

I walked in the door of the apartment and noticed a large group of men playing cards. I looked into the faces of the men and intuitively knew they were military. All I could say to myself was: "God, help me."

Instinctively, I ran for the door. A lot of physical force and violent tempers then erupted. Someone found a rope and tied my

---

[*] Jim Wallis is the editor of *Sojourners* Magazine, Washington, D.C.

hands behind my back. My bag was confiscated, and a group started going through my letters. One of them asked me who I was, and I gave my name. Another shouted: "Karl Gaspar! He is one of them and has a photograph here with us." They all looked at the photograph and then at me. They grinned widely. One jumped up and down and said: *"Promotion na talaga ito"* (this means promotion).

I began to gain courage and demanded my rights: "I have the constitutional rights to seek a lawyer's counsel, to see my family, and to be put in an official detention center."

One of the soldiers got angry and was about to hit me as he said, "What rights?" They then returned to their *piyat-piyat*.

Moments

At certain moments in your life,
the dark clouds take away the light.
You stand naked as the storm engulfs you.
Thunder and lightning underscore
the inevitable gloom.

You find yourself
in the hands of the noonday devil.
You are handcuffed, blindfolded.
Suddenly you realize
the arrest is not just a nightmare.
It is for real.

You are told your rights
don't mean anything.
Scream, but there is no one to hear you.
Run, and that is the end of you.

The moments of agony pass;
in the dawn you
seek the light
and courage.

I was left alone. Then all the fears surfaced: Will they torture me? What forms of torture will they employ? Which safehouse will

I be brought to? Will I be salvaged? Will I survive the night? Will I ever be seen alive again? Prayers followed: "Lord, protect me!"

Just before six, they took me out of the house and informed me that I was to be brought to their officers. Instead, blindfolded and handcuffed, I was brought to a safehouse.

SUNDAY, MARCH 27

The following morning, Sunday, a set of officers came into the room headed by Charlie (the officer who had placed a cloth in my mouth the previous day). The group, according to him, was made up of two other officers who remained silent during the entire interrogation. He informed me that the proceedings were to be taped and I would hear the clicking of the tape recorder.

Charlie was very abrasive and harsh. He would ask questions, but before I could finish answering he would shoot another. He wanted me to rush my answers and not give too much detail. Many times he showed that he did not believe my answers and said that I was just being smart. He implied that I was an infiltrator, a cadre, a subversive, an NDF member, etc. . . . He would then take it all back saying he was just joking. He even justified this joking by saying that some comic relief was needed. Then he left the room, laughing.

None of Your Business

They asked me: why friends call me Karl.
I thought: it's none of your business.
They inquired: why I keep traveling.
It's none of your business.

Except that within such circumstances
it is their business.
Big brother is watching you closely
it is his bloody business.

Blindfolded, handcuffed,
thirsty, hungry, weary;
in fear and trembling
I answered all their questions with fact.

They got angry;
they knew they didn't need facts.
They needed lies.
But I am in the business of truth.

They demanded to know what was my
connection with Kangleon, Tizon, Balweg. . . .*
I was going to say, we're supposed
to be doing the Father's business.
But I really wanted to say:
honestly, it's none of your. . . .

When I realized that I was going to be detained in the safehouse
and that it would be a long and frightening Holy Week for me, I
went down on my knees and asked God's grace to strengthen me, to
keep me calm, and to not let me despair. . . . I realized my position
was very precarious, so I had to come up with something that
would show an offensive stance, that would remind them that I was
a person with rights. I decided that I would go on a hunger strike to
protest my illegal detention and to demand my constitutional
rights. . . . I was to continue this hunger strike all week until Easter
Sunday afternoon. Before I went to sleep I had a prayer reflection
on the liturgy of Palm Sunday. I sang songs, recited my prayers
loudly, and cried as I sought the Lord's grace to make me strong as
I, too, embraced the cross.

MONDAY, MARCH 28

Monday passed and Tuesday came. I continued the hunger strike
which was both a commemoration of Holy Week and an assertion
of my human dignity.

---

* Edgardo Kangleon, a priest from Samar, was arrested Oct. 10, 1982. He died Jan.
4, 1984 as a result of a mysterious car accident which his military driver-escort
survived. Dong Tizon, a priest from Samar, was arrested in Davao in 1983 and was
detained in the same detention center as Karl. Conrado Balweg, an SVD priest
belonging to the Tingan tribe, joined the struggle of his people in the mountains of
northern Luzon in 1979.

TUESDAY, MARCH 29

After lunch a soldier came upstairs to tell me to put on my shoes, for I was to be taken to Manila. . . . In order to make my blindfold less noticeable, they put masking tape on my eyes and over this, sunglasses. . . . At the airport they pulled me out of the car, took me inside a room, put an air force fatigue uniform on me, and placed cotton wool in my ears. It turned out that I was one of more than a hundred soldiers and civilians to board an air force plane. Inside the plane we were made to sit on the railing running along the side. This, along with my being blindfolded, with a bag on my head, and handcuffed, made for a very uncomfortable journey.

When we landed in Manila I was sick as a dog, and when out of the plane I just rolled on the ground. They had to pick me up and push me into a waiting vehicle which took us to a military camp.

At the camp I was put in a room and made to sit on a table. I was so exhausted I again just fell on the floor. . . . They then removed the handcuffs, the bag from my head, the masking tape on my eyes, and my air force uniform. The room, seven-by-ten-by-eleven feet, made of concrete and without windows, was where I was to stay. As there was no bed or mat, I slept on a military raincoat. . . .

Somewhere in Metro Manila

From a safehouse in Davao
I thought I'd be transferred to another safehouse
somewhere in Metro Manila

Instead they dumped me
into this dark, dirty, suffocating cell—a safe cell?
somewhere in Metro Manila

My mind suffocates
at the thought of being held in prison
hardly–safe–at–all
somewhere in Metro Manila

But I know full well,
out there are people who hardly care
except–for–their–safety
they too are in prison
somewhere in Metro Manila.

WEDNESDAY, MARCH 30

The next day, Wednesday, an officer came again to question me, and I was asked basically the same questions they asked in Davao. The rest of the day I just lay down, feeling very hungry, hot, and sick. I was desperate for help and tried to pray and recall songs to sing. I attempted to go on my knees but just rolled over on the floor. At eleven that night another officer came and questioned me until the early hours of Holy Thursday.

This officer proved to be a very kind and considerate soldier. In the next few days I was to see him about twice each day. He saw that I was given a bed and food even though I would not eat. He brought medicine to prevent an ulcer. In my reflection on the way of the cross, he was like Simon of Cyrene.

FRIDAY–TUESDAY, APRIL 1–5

Good Friday and Holy Saturday came and went. I was still there.

Holy Saturday Morning Blues

alone
   in my depressing detention cell

i wonder
   if I'll ever see light at the end of
    the tunnel

across from me
   is an old empty bottle of Johnny Walker
    black label

when the sun
    peaks at noontime
        here it will be as hot as hell

i am about ready
    to collapse into the arms of despair

eight days have passed
    since I mysteriously disappeared

the Christ is in his tomb
    and will soon appear
        in full glory

but i
    will still be here.

On Easter Sunday afternoon the officer in charge of me convinced me to break my hunger strike by promising that on Easter Monday I would "surface."

Easter Monday came. I cleaned my room, washed my dirty clothes, and prepared for the coming of friends. The day passed. No one came.

Easter Tuesday came. Nothing. I cried that night.

SURFACING: LETTERS TO FRIENDS AND BISHOPS

It was on April 9, more than two weeks after his disappearance, that Karl finally surfaced and was visited by his mother and sister. For the first ten days after his capture, the military had denied any knowledge of his whereabouts. His family and friends feared that he was among the many who had been killed in the Philippines. On April 2, possibly because of the national and international pressure exerted on the authorities to account for his disappearance, the military admitted that Karl was its prisoner.

Despite this acknowledgment, it took another week of searching camps in Davao and Manila for the family to actually find him, because in each camp they visited the authorities denied having him.

To Jim Wallis

One of Karl's first letters on surfacing was to Jim Wallis.

In our situation a person is guilty until proven innocent. So I will be detained until God knows when.

But don't worry. I'm okay and in fact I feel privileged with this "gift" of detention. It was very significant that all this happened during Holy Week. I was able to enter into Christ's own experience of agony, despair, suffering, resignation, and hope. And with his grace I was able to embrace my cross fully and survived. . . . Fr. Miguel D'Escoto's statement "We should always be ready to embrace our cross" was the thread running through all my reflections.

I thought of you and prayed for you during my detention just as I prayed for all friends. I remembered our long talk at the tower of that old cathedral in the old section of Geneva. . . . Your kind words helped to keep me strong during my long vigil.

I prayed that you and the members of your community grow in strength and courage to face more crucial tests. . . . Maybe one day you can come to the Philippines so we can have a special issue [of *Sojourners*] on the Philippines.

First "Letter to Friends"

Karl was spared the physical torture inflicted on most political detainees. In his first "Letter to Friends," written on April 9 he reflects on this.

How come the soldiers, both in Davao and Manila, did not physically torture me? Maybe it was because of prayer or because I did not panic and remained calm all through the days of my captivity. When no principle was sacrificed, I tried to be polite and considerate. Or perhaps it was because they perceived me to be "someone." With my master's degree in economics they thought I must be a technocrat. It may also have been the effect of the hunger strike. By the time I reached Manila I was weak and could hardly stand. There would have been no use in torturing me as I was already physically disabled. But I might have been just plain lucky. Who can tell?

But then inflicting physical torture is just one way of extracting information. Mental torture is another form, and in my case this was done through solitary confinement. I was in this very small room. It had no window. The sunshine came through the next room which was a public toilet. It was very hot during the day, and relief came only late at night and very early in the morning. . . . Torture in all its forms is dehumanizing. . . . In the end it was my prayers, my fasting and meditation that rescued me and restored my sense of personal dignity.

Still I don't harbor anger against those who arrested and detained me and subjected me to this frightening sojourn. I have forgiven them, not because they don't know what they are doing, but because they, too, are imprisoned in a system where they have no choice but to follow orders from above. All along the way I was confronted by a hierarchy of terror. The finger always pointed to the guy above. It was frightening to see this in the concrete! No soldier is any longer capable of compassion and human warmth for those in desperate need of it, because the system is devoid of any compassion. That *is* the terror.

Of course there are some fine and gentlemanly soldiers. I met a number of them. But all of them are part of the system! All have positions within the hierarchy of terror which is unleashed on those who dare to challenge the system. The system remains despite the personality of these men.

In the face of all this I had no power at all. They could do with me whatever they wanted. I was perceived to be a man of some education, some social status, some intellectual capacity, and yet I was powerless. What of the simple peasants, workers, tribal leaders, high school kids, and housewives from the squatter areas who have all fallen into their hands. They have no degree, no influence, no backers in government or church, and no friends abroad. Nothing! Christ's own experience was so similar to the experience of peasants and workers who have been detained. There was no lawyer for him; he couldn't cite a Pharisee to intercede for him. . . . One has to undergo the agonizing experience of being a detainee to fully comprehend the frightening implications of our political system and how it operates. One underlying assumption or excuse used by the system is that only communists are showing anger and concern for the plight of the oppressed. It is not believed that we're involved in human rights because of our faith commitment. Nor is it believed that we oppose the U.S. bases because we love our country. We're just instruments through which the communists can advance their activities. This paranoia is becoming extremely suffocating. No longer do they believe there is a communist behind every tree. Now there is one behind every leaf!

I must end here. Again, thank you all for your help, assistance, concern, and prayers. I'm touched by the stories I have heard of what you did in the past two weeks. How can I ever say thank you! All of you, take care, and rage, rage. . . .

To the Bishops of the Philippines

On April 12, Karl wrote to the bishops of the Philippines.

Happy Easter and greetings of peace! By now you must know some of the details of my arrest and illegal detention. . . . The military was hoping that with mental torture I would break down and "confess."

The truth is that I *am not* a top ranking member of the CPP Mindanao United Front Commission. The Resources Development Foundation where I work is *not* "a front for the CPP." My trips abroad were *not* "to contact communists in order to raise funds for the party here." While abroad my companions were usually bishops, priests, sisters and lay churchworkers.

I have told my military interrogators that the reason for my involvement in justice and development issues is my faith-commitment. They cannot comprehend that a faith-commitment would impel us to risk our lives for our brothers and sisters.

Throughout the interrogations it was very clear that the military is concerned about the church. They ask, "Why are bishops, priests, and sisters so antagonistic to the military? Why does the church preach about human rights when this is a political question? Why don't the bishops and priests just concern themselves with spiritual needs and so stop annoying the government?"

I have tried to answer the questions as honestly, objectively, and truthfully as possible. I have always tried to speak from the perspective of the church. It is very clear that the military feels threatened by the church, especially by some bishops. If the military had its choice, no bishop would address himself to human rights.

To the Mindanao Bishops

I have prayed for you all throughout my detention. I prayed: "Lord, if I have to suffer because of my commitment to the gospel, let it be so. Accept this suffering for the Mindanao church and for our bishops. Inspire them and be with them so that they will not harden their hearts to the cry of the poor and oppressed among their flock. May they continue to be prophetic!"

So much has happened since I finished my term at the MSPC three years ago. So many suspicions then, and now the allegations of the military. Some of you may still find it hard to believe that many of us churchworkers are involved with justice because of our faith in the Lord's call "to preach the good news to the poor" and not because of the CPP. Accept my word that this is true. Christ is my witness. He alone was at my side during my own agony.

Please continue praying for me.

THE CASE AGAINST KARL

On April 14, 1983, Karl came before the supreme court. A petition for the writ of habeas corpus *had been filed by Attorney José W. Diokno on March 29. Continued efforts to locate Karl proved futile as the military consistently denied that he was in its custody. Because detainees are frequently subjected to physical and psychological torture in the interval between the arrest and commitment to an official detention center, the petition was filed without delay.*

The supreme court issued the writ on April 4, and all but two of the fifteen members of the court were present for the hearing on April 14. Close to three hundred friends gathered in support of Karl, and he was given an opportunity to greet and talk with them.

Karl was represented by two lawyers. When Chief Justice Enrique Fernando questioned the presence of the two, Karl explained: "I was given no choice but to take Attorney Mateo."

From the beginning of his detention Karl had demanded from

*the military the right of counsel, but the answer of his captors was:
"What right?" Finally when they asked him which lawyer he
wanted to represent him, he said "Attorney Diokno." Karl was,
however offered Attorney Rodolfo Mateo, and, desperate to talk
to a lawyer as he saw this as his only hope of communicating with
the outside world, he accepted the lawyer named by the military.
Karl reasoned that if he agreed to accept Mateo, he would be
surfaced. When asked by the chief justice at the supreme court
hearing whom he wanted to represent him, Karl firmly replied:
"Former senator José Diokno assisted by attorneys Aportadera
and Ilagan."*

The PCO, issued the same day that the habeas corpus *petition
was filed, stated that Karl had "engaged in acts inimical to public
order and national security." Diokno refuted these charges with the
following arguments:*

*1. that Karl was arrested "when he called on an acquaintance,"
and unless "a secret decree has made calling on friends a crime" this
act was not a crime;*

*2. that Karl's illegal arrest had "not been validated by the PCO
issued three days later"; because the issuance of PCOs is limited to
certain crimes, none of which were cited in the PCO in question, it
was invalid;*

*3. that because the PCO did not name any crime or specify what
acts were attributed to Karl that were supposedly "inimical to
public order and national security," it violated basic constitutional
requirements which specify that a warrant of arrest may be issued
only "upon probable cause";*

*4. that the suspension of the writ did not confer upon the
president the power of "preventive" arrest and detention;*

*5. that the manner of Karl's arrest and detention in a "safe-
house" under cruel and inhuman conditions was a violation of his
constitutional rights;*

*6. and finally that since the "military knew they had no case
against Gaspar, they arrested him on mere suspicion, hoping they
could extract a confession from him during detention." In the light
of the national and international protest evoked by his arrest, the
military, to save itself, "sought a PCO, and later concocted . . .
affidavits [which] did not exist on March 29, 1983, when the PCO
was issued. . . ."*

2

Life in Prison

The prison bars and barbed wire that surround a detention center can only imprison the body. A cage may clip the wings of a bird but never its spirit to soar. A prison may reduce detainees' world into a small space, but their capacity to dream will enable them to soar across the limitless sky. Persons can never be fully imprisoned if they can create a world where they can fly with the wings of freedom.

K. Gaspar

Occasionally, in letters to friends, in chronicles, or in seasonal reflections, Karl describes conditions in the detention center as well as the struggle to make a viable community life flourish in the midst of difficult and trying circumstances.

[Dec. 1983] Life in a military detention center is not very comfortable. Anyone in his or her right mind would never opt to live in a place like this! The rooms are limited to cells where the detainees are padlocked for most of their waking hours. The cells are small and congested, and there is hardly any privacy. The beds and the primitive furniture occupy so much space that there is hardly any place to do physical exercise. Lucky are those who do yoga for they only need their bed! Because of the small space and very limited ventilation (only a small open hole near the ceiling), the cells are very warm and humid most of the day and early evening. The lights are inadequate and we don't always have running water during the

13

day. No matter how hard we try to clean the cells, we cannot eliminate the legions of ants, cockroaches, mosquitoes, and even rats.

Within this small space, we eat our meals, do our laundry, read our books and newspapers, play the guitar, listen to the radio, write letters, pray, sleep, stare endlessly at the ceiling, explore ways to make community (no matter how artificial), and serve time.

Still there is so much to be thankful for. There is a roof over our heads, and we are adequately protected from the rain and strong wind. No rent is charged! There is a small space outside where we can sit under the sun and space big enough in which to jog. The women detainees even have a space for a small vegetable garden. But the high barbed wire fence is always there to remind us that we are prisoners of conscience. . . .

Of all the sectors in our society, perhaps the political detainees are the most powerless in the face of the fascist political machinery. Their rights are limited and even those limited rights can easily be ignored. The litany of the violent abuses of detainees' rights includes keeping them hidden in safehouses while the military deny having arrested them, detaining them in solitary confinement with all its ensuing psychological horrors, and torturing them to the point where battered body and shocked brain yield to a nervous collapse. If they are of those called to an early martyrdom, their dead bodies surface along a lonely highway or lie hidden in an unmarked shallow grave. "Salvaging" can take place even after they have been officially detained and a hundred eyes have witnessed to their being "pulled out" (i.e., the practice of *hulbot*).

If they are lucky to survive the horror of their first few days of captivity, they get padlocked with other detainees. Collectively they experience the treatment ordinarily provided criminals.

Visiting rights of family and friends are restricted, conjugal rights are considered a privilege and can easily be denied, and sunnings and other privileges are arbitrarily scrapped. Nonpolitical prisoners share the same cells and they are often made to spy on their fellow prisoners. It is easy to be overwhelmed by the naked display of military might and power and, not surprisingly, rules are accepted without question to avoid arousing the ire of the captors. One cringes at the wrath that the captors are capable of unleashing against the prisoners.

The doctrine of national security justifies the exercise of might by those who have usurped the power of the people. Human cruelty has reached new dimensions of horror due to the pervasive influence of this ideology. Here in prison, any act can be committed by our masters in the name of national security and no one questions it. It is a pretext to crush all dissent and to force everyone to accept the demands of absolute power.

INMATES

[May 1983] There are close to sixty detainees here, but not all are political prisoners since there are three soldiers padlocked with us. In fact there were five the other day but two have since been released. There are around ten Muslim detainees suspected to be BMA members, including the guy who supposedly was involved in the bank robberies in Digos last year. The rest are suspected CPP or NPA top-ranking leaders or members. Still a few are supposedly from the PLM and SocDem groups. The majority are men. There are nine women at present, including a fifteen-year-old girl.

Since we are now more than one hundred detainees, the cells are very congested. This prison should only have fifty prisoners. On the average we are now ten detainees per cell, which should contain only five. The only way to decongest the rooms is by having double-deck beds. The military cannot allot funds for wood and nails, so we asked for outside help. Brother Gene of *Gawasnong Pagbalay, Inc.* (Freedom to Build, Inc.) sent the materials. We all became carpenters. There was a lot of excitement designing the beds and rearranging the rooms. Our cells now look much better with more space in which to move around. Finally in our cell we also have a decent working table. And I am getting a typewriter—what a luxury!

Fear

[May 1983] There are a few here who feel very vulnerable and insecure. They fear something more tragic might still happen to them, even if they're detained here already. This is especially true for those whose parents have not been able to visit them or have come only once or twice. Being peasants, further impoverished by the drought, they can't afford the fare to Davao City to visit their sons. In some cases, relatives are even afraid to come.

The detainees fear the practice of *hulbot* (taking a detainee—who is never seen again—out of the cell in the dead of night). One of the first stories I heard when I arrived here was of a few detainees to whom this happened. We heard later that they were "salvaged." On my fifth day here, an eighteen-year-old kid in my own cell was taken away. We have no idea where they brought him and we were helpless to prevent the *hulbot*. He left with tears in his eyes. Two weeks later his father came to visit him, the second time he had come since his son was detained here. He wasn't informed about the *hulbot* and was made to wait in the visiting area. Fortunately it was our "sunshine session." Those who knew him from his last visit approached him to say that his son was not here anymore! He broke down and wept. . . .

He Is Just a Kid

there was this very young kid
in our cell.
one night he was walking home
the marines saw him
picked him up
tortured him
at one time the torture
got so brutal, he pleaded:
"please kill me."

he was brought to the stockade
just barely a month ago.
his father finally was able
to trace his whereabouts.
he came to visit his son.
that was his only visit
said he couldn't afford the fare.

yesterday the marines
came to take him away.
please don't hurt him,
he's just a kid.

The Commitment of the Poor

[July 1984] In the last month close to twenty new detainees joined us. Almost an entire family was arrested. Apolinar, a fifty-five-year-old worker who lives in a squatter area in the city went up to a barrio with his daughter, his son-in-law, a son, and a prospective son-in-law. They were going to buy bananas, sweet potatoes, coconuts, and bamboo in the countryside when they were picked up by the military for being "subversives." Supposedly they were in the countryside to offer support to the rebels. In the same military operation, a married woman and her sister-in-law were also picked up. Since no one could take care of her three year old son, she brought him here to prison. Now we have a grandfather and a three-year-old detainee! No one is ever too old, or too young, to be victimized by the state's repression against the people. . . .

Most of the detainees here are poor, coming from the peasantry and the working class. If it were not for the FLAG lawyers, many wouldn't be able to get the needed legal counsel to defend them in court. If it were not for the generosity of support groups and the kindness of detainees who are better off, they wouldn't have mats and blankets, soap and cigarettes. If it were not for TFDP, they wouldn't have anyone to follow up their families and look after some of their needs.

Most of those involved in the struggle for justice are the poor. So it follows that most of those who pay the price of that commitment are also the poor. The majority of those who have been arrested, detained, tortured, and salvaged are peasants, laborers, and other PDO. This reality will escalate as the struggle continues.

CITY JAIL

After his transfer to the Ma-a city jail in July 1983 at the height of the hunger strike, Karl wrote of the conditions and population there, comparing the city jail with the detention center at the PC barracks.

The conditions here in the city jail are even more primitive than in the detention center. The sunning schedule is only two or three times a week for twenty minutes. During Sunday Mass, the inmates are kept in their respective cells so there is no opportunity for interaction. Married inmates do not enjoy conjugal rights. The cells are small and congested with an average of twelve prisoners per cell. Water comes from a shallow well, so those with sensitive stomachs get sick easily. Visits of relatives are allowed from Monday through Friday only. The food is inadequate, and there is very limited opportunity for inmates to engage in income-generating activities.

There is great need for reforms here, much more than at the detention center. But the reforms will come only if the prisoners themselves struggle for them. Unfortunately, the inmates here are very difficult to organize. Unlike more of the political detainees who are politicized and easily surrender their own personal comforts for the common good, these prisoners are much more concerned with their own individual interests. The majority of them are from very poor families. This in itself explains why so many are still here. They can't afford good lawyers to follow up their cases and to apply for bail. They are dependent upon lawyers assigned by the court who have little genuine interest in speeding up their release. Because they are poor, they are rarely visited, for relatives cannot afford the transportation. Most are reduced to mendicant status, waiting for visitors to dole out gifts of soap and cigarettes. It is pathetic to see them begging from visitors, but they have no choice.

In time, one gets to know the other inmates, especially those who share the same cell. Many are really good people, not much different from the people one meets among the urban poor communities. Their poverty has dehumanized them. Victimized by unjust systems and structures, they have sought to make money in the only way possible for them. In time, they are caught, but neither this prison nor society provides them the opportunity for rehabilitation. Having experienced how life is in a prison for convicted and suspected criminals, I can see the impact of oppression from another angle. I have become even more convinced of the need for going to the roots of these problems.

A group of charismatics, mainly middle-aged women, comes regularly during the weekend to hold prayer sessions. Their visits spark mixed reactions. On the one hand, they are welcomed by the prisoners for various reasons. They bring biscuits, soap, cigarettes, clothes, and other things needed by the prisoners. For most of the inmates, the charismatics make up for what the relatives cannot provide. Their presence also provides the chance for some socialization.

On the other hand, there is something very disturbing about the kind of Christianity they bring and the gospel they preach. Their prayer sessions have much singing, praising of the Lord, witnessing, and even attempts at speaking in tongues. But no one speaks about the harsh prison conditions. There is no call for social transformation of the oppressive structures of which the inmates are the victims. There are the emotional outbursts asking the Lord for forgiveness and blessings for a new life. But there is hardly any attempt to refer to the Lord in the context of the Magnificat and the Beatitudes.

No wonder their presence here is encouraged by the military authorities. They are being used as instruments to help create a sense of peace and harmony in the prison. They have distributed Bibles, but the most they are able to share is a personalized gospel that has no connection with the real structural problems affecting the prisoners. As Jim Wallis has said in his book *The Call to Conversion*, "the personalized gospel supports the *status quo* because the social meaning of conversion is lost and the proclamation of the Kingdom cannot be heard in its fulness and richness."

FAMILY AND FRIENDS

Many detainees had no visits from family or friends. Karl expresses deep gratitude to those who responded to the needs of these detainees.

[May 1983] We are very dependent on the generosity of family and relatives. Some of us have regular visits and our needs are well cared for. Close to half of the detainees, however, do not have this attention and are dependent on the generosity of the sisters and other kindhearted people who occasionally pass by. Some detainees rarely even see their lawyers, which is another cause for anxiety. . . .

Some of us, however, are luckier than other detainees in terms of having families and friends who help cushion the devastating impact of prison life. From the moment of my arrest, the thought of family and friends sharing the burden of keeping me from harm strengthened me. The least I could do was to pay back the debt by not implicating friends and doing everything possible to avoid harm being done to them. After passing through the most crucial stage of the interrogation, detainees discover that they can actually draw a lot of strength from that wellspring. They have only to dig deeper into the core of their being and trust themselves to be able to tap from that source. I believe all persons have the potential to discover that inner strength if only they will not surrender for the sake of convenience or compromise.

Like a well that draws water from various sources, the detainee draws strength from the concern of others. The love and concern of kin and friends, the encouragement from fellow detainees, reading from the testimony of those who have gone through the same experience and survived, reflecting on the challenging words of the gospel, taking comfort in the thought that evil cannot be in power forever—all of these make the wellspring overflow. While at first detainees are surprised at the gift, later on they realize that it is no big deal. This is especially true as they find themselves in the midst of others who have experienced a far harsher test and who have survived without bitterness or rancor.

. . . I must say that I've come to know more about my family now after a year of seeing them regularly. We have also become much closer to each other.

[May 1984]. . .The generosity of friends continues to touch me deeply. A friend from Australia sent a tape of Victor Jara's songs. I get materials for painting and there's always biscuits and fresh fruits. The books I receive provide a varied collection of good reading material: Leonardo Boff's *Saint Francis*; Albert Nolan's *Jesus before Christianity*; Bienvenido N. Santos's *Distances: In Time, the Portable James Joyce*; Phillip Potter's *Life in All Its Fullness: The Stories of Mbulelo Mzamane; The Health-Introduction to Fiction*; Dorothy Soelle's *Revolutionary Patience*; and Jim Wallis's *Revive Us Again* (which he sent himself). With all the books I've received since I was arrested, I will have a modest library by the time I get released! The only problem right now is that there just isn't enough time to read all the books that come my way. When will we ever find the time to read all the books we want to read if not in prison! What better setting could there be?

My mail continues to yield pleasant surprises, and I must thank those who write for making my mailbag something to look forward to. Sometimes I can't get over the excitement of hearing from long lost friends who have heard about my arrest and detention through circuitous channels. A close friend from college I haven't seen or heard from since 1967 wrote to me from the Trappist monastery in Guimaras. He was making his retreat and while there met another friend now working in Davao. A sister who studied with me in the Asian Social Institute wrote to me from somewhere in Philadelphia after finally getting my address. A student I taught in 1971, who is now a young mother, also recently wrote after hearing about my case from someone she met in Manila.

Then there are the ever-flowing support letters from all over the world, especially Europe, North America, and Australia; they came from Amnesty International groups, church organizations, and human rights advocates. There were, for example, hundreds of postcards that came from a group of four hundred church workers and volunteers who were meeting in Grenoble, France. I also received belated notices informing me of actions undertaken by all kinds of groups to help facilitate my release. Such groups include a football club in Ireland, a justice and peace commission in Japan, a Protestant church congregation in the States, and a Catholic women's league in Canada! God is good and God's goodness is showered on me constantly through old and new friends who offer compassion, comfort, and affection.

To Jim Wallis, Karl wrote of the gratitude and sense of community he felt with the members of the Sojourners community in Washington, D.C.:

. . . And to your community, my special thanks for their prayers. Without having met them I feel a tremendous sense of community with them. It is encouraging to know that in Washington is a group of brothers and sisters that offers prayers for my safety and comfort because I have been accepted as one of them in the spirit of God's love. In turn, a group of political prisoners in a small cell in the deep south of the Philippines remembers all of you in moments of prayer. Despite the great distance that separates us in time and space, in the perspective of the Lord's reign over the universe we are very close. For each of us, our own little world is like the tiny space of the lotus flower. May we always try to discover the tiny space of each other's world for there we will always encounter

> heaven and earth, fire and wind,
> sun and moon, lightning and stars,
> each other everything.

The year of detention and the prayerful concern and solidarity expressed across the miles had brought the two men into a deep and profound friendship. Karl wrote to Jim:

[May 1983] Friendships [in prison] are easily fostered. When new detainees come, the others introduce themselves and the newcomers are encouraged to talk about themselves, their arrests, their cases. Stories are told and retold and there are comparisons of the extent of torture. The new detainees feel welcomed by all the attention. Since there is hardly any privacy in the cells, detainees get to know each other rather quickly and deeply. Problems are shared as people listen to each other pour out the despair that is in their hearts. When tears are shed, comfort is given. When one is depressed, a hand is extended. Compassion and mercy is a way of life here, and it is not very difficult to try to be like St. Francis: "to console, to understand, to love."

[March 1984] I have often reflected that God provided me with "gifts" before I became one of his "suffering servants." One of these gifts is to have met you and to have established our kinship before my arrest. Right now in my long wait for freedom, the words and the spirit we share with each other across the seas provide me with limitless comfort. There really isn't much need for too many words, for in our prayer for each other the kinship continues to blossom and I am blessed.

TENSIONS IN COMMUNITY LIFE

One of the books I read recently was Leonardo Boff's *St. Francis*. It became a humbling experience. I couldn't help but feel so small in relation to the ideal that was Francis. Here I was in a situation where I could see myself unable to take the bold steps toward being an instrument of compassion and concern. When we think our gospel witness is "neatly tucked under our arms," so to speak, then our praxis contradicts us and forces us to take a second look.

[May 1984] It is the season to continue reinforcing the structures of community built over these past months together. Only a sense of community can explain the deep concern we feel for each other. It encourages us to risk seeking a dialogue with the authorities and to go on a fast. This spirit of community, which we celebrate liturgically in a special manner during Mass on Sundays, pervades all our interactions with each other. Whether we are in the garden procuring food for everyone or in our cells tolerating each other's insecurities, we are conscious that we are a community.

Given the psychological pressure that comes with life behind bars, I'm surprised that such a minimum of violence erupts here. If we were all political detainees, it would be understandable. But we have military and suspected criminal detainees here, and we hold very different positions on the ideological spectrum. This alone could provoke tensions. Of course there are occasional fistfights, a number of emotional outbursts, and harsh words now and then, but we have yet to experience a riot. We feel an undercurrent—a few of the military detainees resent the attention given to political prisoners by their friends—but we hope we can maintain the civil atmosphere.

There continues to be a concern for each other's welfare, especially among the political detainees. The ideals of community somehow are more readily practiced in terms of sharing with and caring for one another. It is always a source of amusement to see the younger ones swapping everything from T-shirts to shoes, *malongs* to projects, love letters to lonely moments. They have the flexibility and freedom not to keep things for themselves but to continue sharing with the others. They can teach even the religious how to be a Francis, how to be detached from material things, how to be truly poor and to always be giving from the little that they have. Community fosters generosity, and in prison one can't afford to be selfish.

Our "community life" extends beyond the prison bars to our

relatives and supporters. On days when visitors are not allowed, everyone feels the blues. The sight of relatives is very reassuring and comforting. The visits bring us hope. This is why we try to get to know as many of them as closely as we can and to express our solidarity with them. We will always be grateful to our relatives; without them we would be helpless.

[July 1984] The waiting becomes even more excruciating during anxiety-filled weeks. Such was our collective experience during the past few weeks—a period when Murphy's Law had a heyday! Everything that *could* go wrong *did* go wrong! We are still reeling from the impact of the things that occurred and the anger and frustration that such unfortunate things provoke. Sometimes things happen in prison which bring forth our worst traits. While we try to put up a good front and be considerate and kind toward each other, there comes a time when things don't work out well. These are the times when the lethal combination of boredom, frustration, and despair coalesce in the psyche of a detainee or a group of detainees simultaneously. This leads to the *buryong* syndrome, and when it attacks, problems can arise.

Hardly any maintenance is being done by the authorities in the detention center. The detainees have to fend for themselves with the help of relatives and friends. When beds are needed, we solicit help from outside. The same is true for light bulbs, cleaning materials, carpentry tools, and furniture. Even medicines, reading materials, and similar things are procured through the generosity of friends. The CO says that the government is bankrupt so we shouldn't expect it to provide for our needs. Well, the worst thing happened when the plumbing system of our wing broke down. In a situation where people are padlocked in congested cells, tempers are very short when there is something wrong with the toilets. As we couldn't fix the plumbing system and the CO has no funds, we're stuck with the problem!

Added to this is another unfortunate incident which has increased tension and ill feelings and has resulted in our losing some of our hard won gains. . . .

A jailbreak took place early on the morning of June 9. Al, Arnel, and Dodong managed to get out of their cell after having sawed two prison bars during the sunning sessions. They jumped over the wall at the back where there are no guards or high barbed wire fences and escaped. The three detainees (who were not political prisoners) had been charged with criminal offenses including murder, hold-ups, and illegal possession of firearms and explosives. Out of desperation, they took the risk of escaping from prison rather than spending years in this jail.

They managed to escape before three o'clock in the morning. But two hours later, Al and Dodong were captured, sleeping in the house of the latter's sister. Bruised and battered from the blows they received from the military, they were back with us and padlocked in the *bartolina* before noon. Arnel, however, has still eluded capture.

When the guards and the CO discovered the jailbreak, all hell broke loose. The CO was fuming mad. The first casualty was our newly constructed double-deck beds which our friends had donated. Since the prison bars were sawed off, thanks to the double-deck bed which was used as a base, the CO ordered all double-deck beds dismantled. Our cells had been decongested because of the double-deck beds; now we are back to congestion.

The CO has announced that as "punishment," no visitors will be allowed for a week. The sister of one of those who escaped admitted to providing the saw used to cut through the bars and so the contact between the detainees and visitors is to be restricted. The barbed wire has been moved back, and we are now seven feet from our visitors and have to shout to be heard.

How can there be any privacy with our visitors in such a situation? A new set of rules has also been imposed during sunning sessions: all prisoners must be out of their cells and in the yard even if they are sick. Gardening has been suspended and inspection of things brought in by relatives has become much stricter.

Naturally, the detainees were mad at these new restrictions, but we had no choice but to comply. The detainees' ire turned against the two escapees who need to be escorted out of the *bartolina* when they have visitors, otherwise they would get beaten up. . . .

How long does it take before a detainee loses patience in the face of such an endless stream of problems? How long before prisoners begin to climb the walls out of desperation? How long can the sense of community, which we have fostered, last?

Unfortunately, not too long. In this kind of situation there is bound to be a collision of tempers. Friendships turn sour. Patience falls to its lowest level as friends become less sensitive and more assertive. The dynamics of interrelationships among the detainees become highly charged and some are crushed in the process. We are left with battered hearts, bruised egos, and desolate souls.

We are also frequently left with sick bodies. When the spirit is down, it is not long before virus and bacteria attack the body. The present rash of fevers and colds among the detainees is real but is also probably psychosomatic. . . . I hope I don't bore you with the recitation of our petty travails here in prison. You, too, have your own tribulations to face. While we have hardships, we know that there are hundreds of thousands of people who are in far more tragic circumstances and are able to handle themselves better.

We have certainly discovered our weaknesses in our efforts to help our fellow detainees, especially those who need friendship and support. Life in prison is harsh and everyone gets affected. The eternal lesson, of course, is that we are better able to handle our own problem if we manage to be available to help others resolve theirs. But there are always limits to our capacity. . . .

FREEDOM

A favorite word among the detainees was freedom. *Karl speaks of freedom in his Pentecost letter:*

Laya or freedom is of course the favorite word here. It is at the tip of each one's tongue and is mentioned every other minute. *"Dong, kanus-a ka man molaya?"* (Friend, when will you be set free?) is a question one is continually asked. When one is released, there is collective euphoria as everyone congratulates the detainee about to leave the prison. If you look closely at the eyes of those left behind, chances are you'll see a glint of hope, as they imagine the day they too will have *laya*. Hope springs eternal in the heart of each one.

In a letter of solidarity and encouragement to the Negros Nine [see also pp. 66–68 and 139–141], Karl writes:

I am filled with a sense of solidarity as I write to you from behind our own prison bars and barbed wire, knowing that you will read this behind your own prison bars and barbed wire in the Bacolod provincial jail. But on the other hand, our situation emphasizes the extent of repression in our country, for the prison bars have engulfed all corners of this archipelago. Even those outside the detention centers aren't quite sure whether they are at all freer than we, given the death of freedom in this land.

My codetainees have been following your celebrated case, as reported in the papers, very intensely and with suspense and interest. We admire your action to surrender the privilege of house arrest and to go back to prison in order to share your companions' anguish and anxiety.

. . . We join the hundreds all over the world in praying that you will soon be justly acquitted from this absurd and ludicrous case so that, once more, you will all be free to continue your work of promoting justice and peace.

"Blessed are those persecuted on account of righteousness, for theirs is the Kingdom of Heaven. Blessed are you when they slander and persecute you and falsely accuse you of every wrong because of me" (Matt. 5: 10-11). I thought it very significant that this text was part of the gospel reading last January 29, the very same day that your case was again prominently featured on the front pages of the Sunday papers. Like the prophets, persecuted in former times, you have been subjected to harassment because of your witnessing to the gospel. Along with so many other Christians in our country today who have opted to struggle for justice—including your brother lay leaders who were "salvaged" and buried in that infamous shallow grave in the cornfields of Kabankalan—you have personally experienced the high cost of discipleship.

. . . Your fortitude and strength in the face of tremendous pressure is a source of encouragement for us who also must face and bear our own cross. Since we are all pawns in this national security game, the outcome of your case could have important implications on all those who are victims of the lies perpetrated by the repressive state. If truth is vindicated in the end, then the forces of evil will crumble under the searching light of justice! However, is it realistic to expect that even with the present worldwide pressure the truth will be allowed to surface? After all, this regime can only find its legitimacy in the lies that have become "truth" in the course of their own self-fulfilling prophecy.

Of course we pray that this nightmare will end and that justice will be yours in spite of the judiciary system that operates in our country today. Perhaps there is reason to be optimistic that you shall overcome. After all, have you not the local church of Bacolod, the hundreds of Christian communities in Negros, and thousands of friends and supporters here and overseas with you?

But whatever is the outcome, a prophetic statement has been made. You have shown that you will not be crushed by the intimidating power of your captors. You have inspired us by your sense of community by forsaking privileges in order to protect each other's rights. Your attempt to stick together, to share your common anguish, to be together in your struggle for freedom, all this makes us more sensitive to our own codetainees as we seek to deepen our compassion for the less privileged. In the words of Martin Luther King, written from a prison cell in Birmingham: "You have carved a tunnel of hope through the dark mountain of disappointment." Your hope is our hope.

After months of hearings during which the total inability of the government prosecutors to make the trumped-up charges stick, the Negros Nine were finally released. Karl comments on their release as well as that of Fidel Agcaoili, who served ten years in a Manila detention center before ever being "convicted."

[July 1984] The past weeks brought good news concerning political detainees in other detention centers throughout the country. The first news was that the case against Father Brian Gore and the Negros Nine was dismissed and that they are all released. How welcome this joyful news is. The Negros Nine are finally vindicated and free! Then the supreme court made a decision to end Jose Ma. Sison's (alleged CPP chairman) seven-year solitary confinement. How has this man been able to retain his sanity throughout such a long and torturous punishment? Now we learn that the longest held detainee in martial law history, Fidel Agcaoili, detained for the past ten years, will now be released after having been convicted of his alleged crime. Ten years. How could he also have survived such a long test? It was obviously a face-saving scheme of the regime to convict and sentence him to imprisonment for ten years. Since he has already served it, they will set him free. We, in turn, ask each other the question—can we survive ten years in prison like Fidel and come out of the experience unscathed and without bitterness and rancor?

SOCIAL LIFE

The detainees decided on a social hour to help deepen their own community. Karl writes of one such night:

[Dec. 3, 1983] Earlier this evening we had our "Saturday Night Fever," our second social hour. It went beyond an hour as in October and lasted from 6:30 to 8:30 P.M. There were songs, poems, dances, and comedy skits. After the display of talents, we had a dance. Just as most of us got exhausted with the dancing, it began to shower. Since we held the affair out in the open space, it was the right time for the guards to call it a night. Now we're padlocked again in our cells but grateful for the break.

It was not without a trace of guilt and a feeling of absurdity that we decided to push through with this social hour. Edgar from across our cell said: "How can we afford to sing and dance when the detainees in Manila are now fasting to demand that ALL political detainees be freed?" A few also felt that with the sea tragedy* (in fact we will hold a memorial Mass tomorrow), we should be in a spirit of mourning rather than having a good time. All this, along with the worsening economic crisis and the woes chorused by our visiting relatives, made our night of fun and frolic seem frivolous.

But I guess we are all so starved for occasions to socialize with one another that any opportunity that arises is grasped tightly. One precious evening to be out in the open and to gaze at the stars in the stillness of the dark night is awaited with intense enthusiasm and, when it is offered, can hardly be rejected. It brings a touch of the outside reality and somehow for over an hour we feel light and cheerful.

---

* See chapter 3, pages 59–60 for a description of the tragic sinking of the M/V Cassandra which claimed the lives of seven religious women, one priest, and several lay church workers.

This enjoyable evening was also a spontaneous *despedida* for Virgie who might be released in custody on Monday. Virgie is five months pregnant and it would be very convenient for her and the coming baby to be out of prison. But poor Nathaniel will be left behind, although he too is glad his wife will be released.

Life in prison is always much more difficult for those who are married and have children. Over one-fourth of the detainees here are married. Apart from Virgie and Nathaniel, there is another married couple here in prison. One is always moved by the pain etched on the faces of wives, especially those who are pregnant, when they come to visit their husbands. This Christmas season, the wives of two codetainees will give birth. There will be two Christmas *niños* whose first cry after birth will be a plea for their fathers' release. As the event is about to occur, one hears the men wishing that they could be at their wives' side at the moment of birth.

Before our social hour ended, one detainee asked whether such an hour is allowed to the prisoners in other detention centers. We didn't know but we hope it is. But then such privileges come only after a struggle where the detainees themselves demand more humane treatment. As I write this letter, a few are still awake recalling the highlights of the evening's affair (like schoolboys wondering how their play or chorus performance went), and they are already dicussing what to present in the next social hour. It seems rather absurd that our preoccupation now is the pursuit of fun and enjoyment when just a few months ago we lay down on the floor, hungry and emaciated, wondering whether the hunger strike [see chap. 5] would succeed in breaking down our captors' hold around our necks.

PRISON THEATER

Memories of past years in theater work were revived for Karl as he worked with his fellow detainees to stage a short musical play during one of the monthly social nights.

[Mar. 1984] In order to provide more relevant content for our monthly social hour, we managed to get permission to stage a subtly anti-imperialistic short musical play entitled *"Bayabas ni Juan"* (Juan's guava tree), a classic piece in the repertory of many local theater groups. A compact historical play, it chronicles the Spanish invasion and American domination of the Philippines. Its power lies in its comic and satirical nuances, which explains why we were allowed to stage it. We set up a seventeen-person drama troupe, sought permission to rehearse together for a week, staged it with even the prison guards amusingly joining in the crowd's guffaws, and assessed the activity as a cultural breakthrough! For myself, it brought back memories of the years of theater work and a sense of fun at directing amateur actors who were just discovering the power of using the body to communicate a relevant message.

LIMITS OF YOGA

[Mar. 1984] One of the first books that I received after I was surfaced and allowed a visit with my family was a book on yoga which my *a te* [elder sister] gave me. I had always wanted to try yoga but, before my arrest, the frenetic pace I kept somehow got in the way of doing it. Now I finally had the time and the setting. I am glad I got into yoga for it has certainly helped keep me fit physically and mentally through this past year. Along with jogging it has helped to keep away mental stress, a syndrome which one can easily spot among the detainees. Of course it is easy to understand why mental stress would be as common as the common cold among those caged in prison cells.

Yoga and jogging, however, are not enough to combat the depressing impact of mental stress. Something else is required and one doesn't need to look too far to discover what that is. In the world outside it is a known fact that there are a far greater number of people affected by mental stress in highly industrialized urban centers, where alienation and isolation have made the people more concerned with caring for their individual needs rather than for the needs of the other.

That "something else" is in *the* "Book" that speaks about love of neighbor, loving the least of our brothers and sisters, sharing each other's burdens, being one in mind and heart as well as living in community where there is sharing of joys and pain. One will not escape the bottomless pit of mental stress by falling into the abyss of selfishness! One will escape the quicksand of nervous collapse only if the hand is extended to others who need empathy and support. Francis, who spoke of being able to receive only through giving, knew this only too well.

Fortunately, in a detention center, where most of the detainees are political prisoners whose concern and compassion for others has been internalized through years of commitment, there is a contagious spirit of camaraderie.

COMMITMENT

Karl ends one of his earlier letters with a reflection on the agelessness of commitment. His thoughts were sparked by the death of a school administrator in his late sixties and the renewed contact with a seventeen-year-old student activist who wrote to comfort Karl in the loss of someone who had been a friend to both of them.

[Aug. 1983] As I finish writing this letter I remember two people who are a source of inspiration for me. One is a sixty-seven-year-old school administrator and the other a seventeen-year-old student. Despite the fifty year gap between them, they share one common dream: to see this country fully freed from poverty and oppression. Both, in their respective sectors, were committed to participate in the growing national movement for justice. These two people are proof that one is never too old or too young to become involved. Unfortunately, the administrator was recently killed in an accident.

The day he was buried I received a note from the student. I remembered how I used to carry her when she was just a five-year-old girl and we were first attending rallies and demonstrations in Manila in the premartial law days. Now she is a student at the state university, and I heard from her father that she was a committed activist. Her short note to me was an attempt to provide comfort and consolation. I needed it badly that day as I prayed for the eternal peace of the school administrator. She said: "*Kuya*, don't worry, we shall go on. Those in power rule now, but one day they will fall. One day we will be liberated!" Echoes of the Magnificat coming from a seventeen-year-old girl trying her best to provide courage in what is now a reversal of roles!

At that moment I was struck by the juxtaposition of the images as I placed the faces of the school administrator and the young student side by side: life and death, youth and maturity, hopes and griefs, sunrise and sunset. These are the cycles of life which govern our existence even as we dream of a kingdom that has been announced, but that is still to be fulfilled. In the lives of these two people, the cycles continue but the dream remains. This is the dream of a people to be free to determine its own destiny and to mold its own society of justice and peace.

May we remain faithful to this dream forever, as we seek God's blessing to help us attain it in due time.

Harvest time at the detention center brought vegetables to supplement the detainees' meager diet. The idea of the harvest season suggested to Karl a season for summing up and taking stock of gains made through collective actions taken.

[May 1984] It is the season for harvesting. Yesterday morning a group of us were in the garden at the back of the detention center. It had rained the previous evening, so the garden looked very fresh and the fertile ground was wet. As the early morning sun rose from the east, little white flowers which sprout from the many weeds glistened in the sun's warm glow. The *narra* trees that grow just outside the fence that separates us from the outside world were in bloom, their fragrant yellow flowers emitting a scent that is associated with bright happy mornings.

Indeed it was a bright, happy morning as we harvested vegetables which we had planted a few months ago. There was a feeling of utter joy that pervaded the atmosphere as we started to harvest the fruit of our labor: fresh radishes, *petchay, camote tops,* eggplant, and tomatoes. Somehow the productivity of the good earth was so reassuring. Here was life within our circumstances; this was life in its fresh abundance. With a very limited budget for food, the vegetables we were able to gather were welcome since the authorities can't afford to buy sufficient food for all of us. Our harvest supplements whatever little food is served us. Yesterday, to celebrate the harvest, we contributed toward the purchase of fish and we had *kinilaw*!

It is the season for taking stock of our gains as political prisoners and to push one more step toward humanizing our condition.

Almost a year has passed since our hunger strike [see chap. 5].
While prison conditions have improved because of that mass action, our life here is no picnic. So much still needs to be done to
make the conditions more humane. After consulting with one
another we struck again, to the consternation of the authorities.
However, we had learned some lessons last year on how to go about
asserting our rights. This time the process was less antagonistic.
Rather we were conciliatory and charming, taking pains to consider the nuances of culture and always trying to avoid putting
Colonel Valderama, the MetroDisCom chief, on the defensive.

First we wrote him a letter thanking him for keeping his word
about implementing our terms of the agreement with him, which
ended last year's hunger strike. We then asked him for a dialogue to
discuss "areas of concern"—we refrained from using the word
"demands"—at his earliest convenience. These included the following requests:

1. An increase of our food allowance from six to twelve pesos per
day per detainee (with the two devaluations in the past year and the
double-digit inflation what can one buy with six pesos these days?);

2. The release of those whose cases have been dismissed in court
as well as the minors;

3. For our Sunday visitors to stay until noontime so we can have
more time to entertain them after Mass;

4. The extension of visiting time from thirty minutes to an hour;

5. An end to the practice of taking detainees out for investigation
(in some cases to undergo torture again) without the knowledge of
relatives and lawyers;

6. That the use of the *bartolina,* the dark dirty room meant for
solitary confinement purposes, be stopped;

7. The disciplining of prison guards who inflict physical harm on
detainees;

8. The dismantling of the barbed wire fence that separates us
from our visitors in the visiting area;

9. The improvement of the surroundings, especially the need to
fill up the compost pit at the back.

It was almost a week before he responded and only because our
action was reported in the papers. We had agreed with the support
groups that there be no media coverage of our request for dialogue,
knowing the chief's "allergy" to news accounts involving his com-

mand. But the enthusiasm of our supporters cannot be controlled at times so, like the chief, we too were surprised when our proposed dialogue was reported by the local Sunday papers. He was furious and for a moment we thought it would spoil the planned smooth process. It turned out to be a blessing in disguise. He came to the dialogue in his jogging outfit and even missed his breakfast.

The two-hour dialogue wasn't much of a dialogue though because, ordinarily, military officials do not have the patience and sensitivity to listen, so they end up talking to themselves. Still we managed to tackle the "areas of concern," which ultimately became "demands." Except for the dismantling of the barbed wire he approved the demands in principle. He then asked his CO to meet with a representative group of detainees—whom we chose—to discuss the mechanics of the implementation. That evening Lt. Villaroman sat down with us in order to discuss the mechanics. That was how the dialogue ended. It wasn't a roaring success—most of the "granted" demands still have to be implemented as of today—but neither was it an exercise in futility. Apart from the excitement and drama involved in a mass action right in the belly of the beast, we showed them we will never simply acquiesce to their manner of handling us.

AN IMPRISONED SOCIETY

[July 1984] As I chronicle the main events here in prison, . . . I realize the many limitations involved in explaining to you, my friends, the human drama that we all experience. There is only so much that one can write about because of certain realities. I am afraid I have a tendency to exaggerate some facets of our life here at the expense of other angles. It is not my intention to paint such a bleak scenario in order to seek pity. By my sharing some vignettes of our life under detention, perhaps you will be able to see that our situation mirrors that of the broader Filipino society, which is just one huge prison because of oppression and repression. There are tremendous injustices inflicted on political detainees. Their voices cry out to heaven for an end to their unjust captivity. There must be an end to the existence of detention centers for prisoners of conscience. There shouldn't be any political prisoners. Any society that condones, let alone promotes, the setting up of political pris-

ons deserves its own demise. It stands in need of a radical restructuring so that no person need fear being padlocked in such a gaol as
this on the basis of political beliefs and options.

How long, Lord, will it take for your kingdom to come? How
long before we can glimpse the dawning of a just and humane
society that will foreshadow your kingdom? How long will we
wander in the desert of our suffering and struggle before we reach
the threshold of our own promised land?

3

Reflections on the National and International Situation

What meaning has life if we do not have a land where we can be carefree and wild; if we do not have songs that allow the soul to burst out in celebration; if we do not have a country and a people to call our own?

K. Gaspar

Karl became a keen observer of national and international events as they unfolded, and reflections on these events were included in many of his letters.

[March 1984] Many times we find ourselves in the thick of history's unfolding. In fact, our sense of history at some moments has been quite overwhelming. It is exciting to be caught in the historical flow of events even if we are but at the periphery of such incidents. Political detainees all over the country have been making history by the sheer power of their survival. They are occupying a prominent place in the nation's consciousness despite the regime's propaganda that there are no political detainees. Their collective voice has not been stilled, for even their silence echoes in the hearts of those who care about freedom. As long as we remain in jail, there can never be peace in the land. Because human rights are violated, the nation is bleeding and we are the living testimonies. . . .

REFLECTIONS ON A SILVER ANNIVERSARY:
LETTER TO HCCD

Twenty-five years. When we look back, we wonder what happened to all those years. Yet the memories of those early years remain vivid. The year 1959 is like a lifetime ago, for so many things have happened between 1959 and 1984. In the context of the realities and events of today one can become very nostalgic about those early years. Given the heavy responsibilities we face today as adults, there is a longing to bring back those years when HCCD was like a big playground in a neighborhood where carefree young boys nurtured dreams for peace and prosperity. . . .

On this the twenty-fifth year since HCCD's founding, I find myself behind bars and barbed wire. I would like to believe that it is not just by a quirk of fate that I am here in prison. I would like to believe that the long and winding road that I have taken through these years which has brought me here as a prisoner of conscience really started at Sacred Heart Avenue. In 1959 it was a dirt road. I remember that whenever there was a heavy rain, Sacred Heart Avenue would be so flooded that classes were suspended. The announcement of course was to our heart's delight, for we would spend the day inside the nearby theater!

Now, in this congested, dark prison cell, as I try to recall the highlights of my school years, a few faces and events stand out. The passage of years makes the memories rather hazy at times, and certainly they no longer come in chronological order. But they remain in my mind and they keep me anchored to a past which certainly provides a strong foundation for the principles I hold sacred. As I greet you on your silver anniversary, let me share these images with you.

In 1962, we were in fourth year. In one religion class that year, Brother Clement (who was our beloved guru and class adviser throughout our four years) said something which proved to be very prophetic. He said that the situation of poverty in the country was worsening. If nothing happened by way of alleviating the people's impoverished condition, there would be a social conflagration in ten years' time. In spite of the fact that I was then so politically naive, his words sank very deep in my unpoliticized consciousness.

In 1972, ten years later, martial law was declared. On the night that martial law was inflicted on the Filipino people, the house where I was staying in Mati, Davao Oriental, was raided by a PC squad and three of us were arrested and imprisoned in the PC barracks. When Brother Clement spoke of what would happen in ten years' time, I'm sure he did not envision martial law and its concomitant evil. When I sat there listening to his prediction—which I thought was rather foreboding and pessimistic—it never occurred to me that I would be in the eye of the storm ten years later.

It is now 1984 and the nation's scenario is even more foreboding and desolate. The economic crisis has further intensified and I'm sure, like many Catholic schools, you are on a tightrope not knowing how long you can survive the hard times. The political scene is not very rosy either, and Davao del Sur has become one of the most heavily militarized provinces. The events of the past year have shown how serious the instability of our political economy is, how widespread the social unrest is, and how insecure is our future as a nation!

I remember Elmo Cagape. He was a part of the class of 1963. He was not in my *barkada* [group] so I wasn't close to him. But I remember him as a kind and helpful person. He was one of those quiet students, not making much trouble for anyone, always considerate of others. I cannot remember now when I last saw him, but I remember very distinctly how I felt when I heard the news that he was salvaged. According to the rumors, he was killed by the military because of his connections with the underground. Unfortunately, there was never a thorough investigation of his death, so the truth has never surfaced. What really happened to Elmo?

If he was killed by the military on suspicion that he was a subversive, then Elmo rightfully belongs to history as one of our contemporary martyrs. The class of 1963 could rightfully claim the honor of having one in our midst who died so that others might live in a land where justice reigns. If his death was but an accident, then he was one of the countless victims of a regime which has a very low regard for life. In either case, Elmo was one of the first to be salvaged in Davao del Sur.

A few years after Elmo's death, Digos was to figure prominently on the front pages of the national and local newspapers because of the salvaging of three young men who were later buried in a common, shallow grave in the town cemetery. Because of the IBP's militancy, this case was brought to national attention along with other similar incidents. Davao del Sur is now in the consciousness of the country because of such appalling human rights violations.

In 1970 I came again to HCCD and spent a few months there while helping Bishop Francisco Claver, S.J., gather data for his doctoral thesis in the barrios of some towns of Davao del Sur. A year later, when I had joined the faculty, I went to the countryside with some students to gather data for a socioeconomic profile of the province needed as a document for the PAASCU accreditation. Having grown up in the *poblacion,* I had very little exposure to the countryside, no matter how near we were geographically to the barrios. These two occasions provided me an opportunity for a deeper immersion in the barrios of Davao del Sur.

The poverty and deprivation of the peasants in the countryside makes one despair. Nearly everything works against them: the feudal land ownership patterns, the incursion of plantations on land meant for cash crops, the collusion between land-hungry bureaucrats and the military, the poor infrastructure of farm-to-market roads and bridges, the lack of credit and marketing assistance, and the like. As a result, the specter of death hovers over their wretched lives. A slow death that comes with malnutrition has given way to an institutionalized violence that devours the poor and powerless. The number of the victims has become disturbingly high.

As I went through the barrios of Davao del Sur, I was struck by the seeming hopelessness and helplessness of the people. Is it a surprise, therefore, that today those same barrios are hotbeds of dissent in Davao del Sur? Despite the censorship of news, some reports manage to come out of Davao del Sur that show a pattern of widespread guerilla activity and an increasingly politicized base which supports the insurgence. It is with great difficulty that the military attempts to check the ever-widening growth of dissent. These are signs of the times, but are we able to discern our response as Christians?

I remember Teresita "Tiray" Marasigan. She was my student in an economics class I taught in HCCD during the First Quarter Storm. I was close to her family, and she was like a younger sister.

She was a very bright student who used her brains, not so much to pursue academic excellence as to discover the historical and structural roots of her people's oppression and to discern what should be done to radically change society.

Her search for meaningful involvement in the people's struggle brought her to the countryside where her option was further reinforced. She paid a dear price for such an option. She was arrested and jailed as a political detainee along with her best friend, Mae. But she didn't give up because of this difficult interlude. As a detainee she saw what could still be done by lawyers if they would come to the defense of those whose rights were blatantly violated. So she took up law. Had it not been for that tragic road accident she would have been a lawyer by now. Who knows, she might have taken up the case of her former teacher and have become my legal counsel!

HCCD during the First Quarter Storm wasn't really such a major hotbed of student radicals, but we did have a few. Their faces are a little blurred now and I don't know whether I would still recognize them if I met them on the street. Most have chosen to join the establishment and have married. They are now safely ensconced in their chosen professions. Like many HCCD alumni they are everywhere: banks, schools, government services, insurance companies, and family businesses. The alma mater has reason to be proud of their successes. But what is a successful alumnus? What are the criteria used in singling out outstanding alumni? I'm afraid Tiray and her kind wouldn't quite make it. But maybe one day the alma mater will pay tribute to Tiray and her kindred spirits. . . .

ASSASSINATION OF "NINOY" AQUINO

On August 21, 1983, Senator Benigno "Ninoy" Aquino was assassinated upon his arrival at the Manila International Airport.

[Aug. 30, 1983] I wanted to write some thoughts on Ninoy. News of his assassination reached us here in prison on the day after it happened. My mother came on Monday morning and told us about it. What was your reaction when you first heard it? For myself, I naturally was shocked. Then I thought: an era is finally closed.

Ninoy's death ended that era dramatically. During that era we had pegged our dreams on the existing political structure and had expected it to live up to our ideals of democracy. These ideals we would now label as reformist or even reactionary, but when we were sixteen or eighteen we didn't hear those words.

Tomorrow they will bury Ninoy's body. Then what will happen? Perhaps Ninoy is the sacrificial lamb and his death will pave the way for national reconciliation and democratization. Like Pinochet in Chile, Marcos may really bend over backwards to bring back civil liberties and freedoms. Will the nonviolent third force stage a big leap forward and mobilize the silent majority, or is Ninoy's bloody death a sign that the violent confrontation between the established elite and the people will increase? Will his murder lead to an increase of repression that could result in a *coup d' état*? . . .

[Sept. 8, 1983] "Lord have mercy on us. We have put our hope in you" (Isa. 33:2). It is more than two weeks now since the assassination of Ninoy Aquino. Even though we are cut off from the larger society with its channels and avenues of communication, we can still feel the impact of his death. Like everyone else, we wanted a substantial media coverage of the events surrounding the murder. The local media's coverage is so sketchy; and we have been struck by the attempt to limit the coverage. Friends who write give their prognosis of the coming crucial weeks: either greater repression or a move toward democratization. Which way are we going? Right now there seems to be a dramatic shift in the scenario.

Aquino's assassination cries out to heaven for justice! The regime has tried to salvage its credibility by pointing its finger at local communists as the ones responsible for the dastardly act. The president has cried wolf again! But ordinary Filipinos, and that includes nearly all the prisoners here, have made up their minds who the real criminal is, and no matter how hard the controlled media try to absolve the government, no one believes them anymore. So many lies have been told the people all through these years of martial law that very few give the state the benefit of the doubt. John Paul II says: "The lie is at the root of violence, and the search for truth is the work of peacemakers." The monumental turnout of people during the wake and funeral is symbolic of both the search for truth and the rage of people who will no longer tolerate the abuses of the government and the military.

Lord, how many more of our people will shed their blood so that justice and peace may reign in our troubled land? How many more widows and orphans will shed tears at the murder of their loved ones by the forces of evil that continue to dominate the structures of power? When will we stop weeping at the senseless misery that surrounds us? Is there no end in sight to the brutality inflicted on your people in our besieged and tormented land? Hear our lamentation, Lord, and listen to our cry for justice!

The murder of Aquino seems to have been the turning point for large numbers of the middle and upper class who, for the first time since martial law, began to take to the streets in the large cities. This weekly event came to be called Yellow Friday.

[Oct. 28, 1983] It is Yellow Friday! As I write this letter, we are listening to a local radio station's coverage of the Yellow Friday protest festivities in the main streets of Davao City. As in the past two Fridays, thousands of people are joining the "confetti revolution." We, too, can feel the electricity in the streets, thanks to the radio coverage. Since we're padlocked in our cells, almost everybody is glued to the radio listening to the detailed description of the happenings in the streets. . . .

While Yellow Fridays bring the fiesta atmosphere to the streets even as the demonstrators call for Marcos's resignation and an end to tyranny, here in the detention center, it might as well be Blue Friday. It is standard operating procedure for the military to be on red alert whenever there is a rally or demonstration outside. This means no relatives are allowed to visit us, and we are not allowed our sunning session. So we remain padlocked in our cells. It is frustrating to be cut off from such events and to be reduced to the role of a bystander or a mere listener to radio broadcasts while history is unfolding in the streets.

The Yellow Friday street demonstrations as well as the prayer rallies, marches, and other activities which have mushroomed all over the country following the August 21 tragedy have become sources of optimism for us. These popular expressions of the people's discontent and dissent have further intensified the call for national reconciliation. Practically all the groups and organizations linked to the Justice for Aquino, Justice for All movement (JAJA) have included a plea for a general amnesty for political offenders and the subsequent release of all political detainees as an integral move toward national reconciliation. . . .

The growing clamor from all sectors for the freeing of all political detainees is our new source of hope. It has brought about an air of optimism throughout the detention center, and it dovetails with the sense of camaraderie which developed after the hunger strike, not only among the detainees but even with most of our guards. Both the hunger strike and the post-August 21 events have contributed towards breaking down the oppressive restrictions. The climate here is now less tense and more human. Our relatives are no longer subjected to harassment and insult. We can now interact more freely with the women detainees during common sunning sessions and Sunday Mass. Practically all relatives and friends are allowed to visit us, except for foreigners, perhaps due to the regime's antagonism to the Western press aggravated by the Aquino assassination. . . .

The dramatic change in our situation here inside corresponds to the significant developments outside. Like many others, we are overwhelmed with the new force in the streets, especially with the seething anger of the middle class and the martial law babies. We are struck by the heightened courage of the opposition, the human rights advocates, and even some local media people. We are impressed by the popular movement's sustained and even increasingly influential drive to push for the people's democratic rights. We are touched by the widespread concern for our release.

In the two months that have followed Ninoy Aquino's murder we, too, can sense that the country is experiencing a turning point. Most of our lawyers are with the JAJA so they update us when they come for visits. We now kid ourselves that with the coming amnesty we will all be out of here before Christmas!

AQUINO'S BIRTHDAY

[Nov. 27, 1983] Today is Ninoy Aquino's birthday, and all over the country there are prayer rallies, marches, and demonstrations which have been organized by JAJA and its local counterparts. In

Davao City, there was a march this afternoon which culminated in a rally at the city plaza, between the city hall and the cathedral. The demands of the march and rally are the same everywhere: the end of tyranny and militarization, the restoration of the people's constitutional rights, the resignation of Marcos, freedom for all political detainees, the truth behind Aquino's murder, and free and honest elections in 1984.

Relatives of the detainees marched as one group and carried banners and placards demanding our release and the declaration of general amnesty. My mother, brothers, sister, nephews, and nieces were in the march. My mother isn't exactly a young, slim, athletic woman, so the five-kilometer march must have been an ordeal for her. But since I got arrested she's become a veteran of protest marches and mass mobilizations. What mothers won't do for their beloved sons!

Further reflection on the assassination of Aquino and its aftermath are contained in a chronicle written in November–December 1983:

[Nov. 30, 1983] The murder at MIA last August was the straw that broke the camel's back. Aquino's assassination underscored the extent to which the regime will go to devour those who would oppose its legitimacy. The blood that was spilled on the tarmac mingled with all the blood shed by the martyrs in search of justice and freedom. . . . Their presence is felt as their names are reverently mentioned in prayer rallies and mass mobilizations. They symbolize the people's hope to tear apart the fear and indifference that are the result of long years of acquiescence to the dictatorship.

It is almost four months since the social unrest blossomed, sparked by the people's wrath in the aftermath of that killing. Their protest continues to unfold on the streets, and the voice of the people refuses to be silenced; their songs now penetrate even the enclaves of the elite. Now it is autumn. The dictatorship is dying and the cracks in the fascist wall are widening.

Despite the restriction of being in prison, our spirits are high. We are encouraged by the hundreds of thousands of people throughout the country who have further intensified the call for structural change. We don't mind the long wait behind bars and barbed wire because there is now a multitude who are out to dismantle the chains that have made all Filipinos prisoners in their own country.

It is inspiring to read the documentation of this new upsurge of activism. The words of a businessman in a rally in Makati bring us hope: "Today we cannot afford to be silent. Without provocation, we must speak out. Without fear, we must bring out the truth. Without hope, we will strangle. But with courage and confidence in truth and justice, we shall overcome."

[Aug. 17, 1984] It is now a year since Ninoy was murdered on the tarmac of Manila airport. His death has been a turning point in our contemporary history, a galvanizing factor in regard to the rise of popular dissent. This is especially true for the middle class in the urban centers, the greater number of whom had been hopelessly apolitical and indifferent. That sector, however, is vacillating by nature so it is not surprising that they are quieter after a year of Ninoy-inspired confetti rallies and yellow marches. The radical syndrome invaded Makati and other pretentious urban centers, but those who were swept into this tide were still far removed from the life and death struggle of the countryside.

Where are we now a year after that event? As a people, we are wiser. We know that the U.S.-Marcos dictatorship cannot be dismantled solely by Yellow Fridays and asking Marcos to resign. We are poorer. The economy has further deteriorated, despite the help given by the U.S. to keep it from collapsing, and we are on the verge of mass hunger. We remain gripped by fear. The repressive decrees are still operative, national security remains an obsession on the part of the state, and human rights are dispensable. In spite of the paralyzing fear, more and more people have broken out of the culture of silence and are out on the streets crying out their protests, raising their clenched fists, and signing their militant songs.

We still have a long way to go before we can achieve justice, freedom, and democracy. We are still in the darkness of our collective outrage, and we are shedding tears and blood as we assert our right to self-determination. Through all this, "we have trust in life because this night will pass and a new day will dawn. We have trust in life because we do not have to live through it alone. God is with us!" (Alfred Delp, S.J.).

THE ECONOMIC CRISIS

The last half of 1983 witnessed an alarming downward trend in the economic situation. This was exacerbated by the assassination of Aquino.

[April 7, 1984] These days the people are much poorer as a result of the twin devaluations, the skyrocketing prices of basic commodities, and the declining value of their income due to severe inflation. As the economy totters on the brink of collapse, the government's response to stave off bankruptcy is to incur more loans to add to its gigantic $25.6 billion foreign debt. The people are far more insecure with unemployment rising, an increase in crime, and a sense of malaise spreading like a cancer. The escalating militarization in the countrywide and the repressive presidential decrees have further emphasized the fascist character of this regime that has brought more oppression to our people. Meanwhile with more U.S. military aid being poured into the regime's coffers, the military has sought to win hearts and minds even as it has tortured countless persons and dumped bodies of salvaged victims in shallow graves. . . .

[May 1984] It is the season for a new cycle of hardship and despair for the poor—and even among an increasing number of the urban petty bourgeois—as the regime recently announced a 10 percent increase in gasoline prices. Following the elections in which the oppositionists were allowed to share a bigger piece of the pie, the euphoria of the middle class dissipated with the new wave of skyrocketing prices of prime commodities. To add insult to injury, not only are prices of goods exorbitantly high, but goods are nowhere to be seen because of the uncontrollable hoarding. People are indignant, but it will still take a little while before the majority will understand that the regime has made the people captives of the IMF-WB clique, and that our close to $30 billion* external debt has made us subservient to imperialist interests.

---

* The official figure was $25.6 billion, but other sources reckoned that the debt was closer to $30 billion.

The new round of increase in prices is bad news for everyone. Relatives who come to visit us are burdened by it and we naturally are affected. Because of the increase in transport fares, many relatives can't visit their kin here as often as they did in the past. They are also apologetic about food gifts they bring. The current joke is the good news–bad news contrast regarding our demand for an increase in food allowance: the good news is that there's been an increase from 6 to 8 pesos per day per detainee; the bad news is that 8 pesos is now worth only 4 pesos. *Kasakit!* [How painful!] Since we are not able to increase the selling price of our crafts, we also can't afford to increase our labor share, so our small income becomes even smaller in value. Another joke here is the suggestion that we could go on strike. The problem is that we are also the management, so we will be on a strike against ourselves.

[July 9, 1984] We are really in the worst of times! The 40 percent inflation rate, the peso devaluation, the massive unemployment, the rising cost of living, the poverty and misery—all these affect us as much as they do our relatives and friends outside. The daily collective lamentations of our families about high prices and low incomes bombard us during visiting hours. We feel so helpless because we can't do anything to help. A few even feel pained that they only add to the family's burden since precious money is spent on transportation and other expenses when family members come to visit. We still eat three meals a day, but there are no more eggs or meat. Our meals are rice and fish, and it is the lowest quality of rice and fish sold in the market.

This situation is most difficult for the indigent young boys and the married among the detainees. There is no way the voracious appetite of these growing kids can ever be satisfied with the limited food available, even if all is shared. My heart goes out to a seventeen-year-old kid here named Charlie whose mother only visited him once since he was detained three months ago. He longs for the day when she will be able to come back and visit him again and perhaps bring his favorite dish. It is hard for the married detainees to be in prison, as they worry whether their children are still able to eat and go to school.

The economic crisis has also caught up with crafts project. Despite the limited income earned by detainees, about 100 pesos per month, it has been useful to pay day-to-day expenses, especially for the indigent prisoners. In some cases, this income has helped in the transportation costs incurred by relatives who come to visit and even to help in the school expenses of siblings. Apart from income earned, the project has also served to counter boredom. Unfortunately, our external support system for the marketing of these products is not well organized; our capitalization is limited and cannot sustain continuous production. Local sales have plummetted because people's income now goes chiefly to food and basic necessities. We have had to declare a moratorium until we get our present inventory sold out.

U.S. IMPERIALISM

The following letter was addressed to the Maryknoll Sisters of the Philippine region, most of whom are from the U.S.:

[April 1984] Reagan, the U.S. State Department, the CIA, the IMF-WB, Armacost, and everyone else in the clique have, in the last few weeks, denied interference in the internal affairs of this country. Despite the denials, most Filipinos know they are lying. The U.S. military bases and the more than $2 billion economic interest of American TNCs here are BIG reasons why the U.S. interfered with the state of Philippine affairs. Even Marcos attacks such interference, but who is he kidding, when he desperately needs the $630 million loan from the IMF-WB, the continuous patronage of Reagan, military aid, foreign investments, and everything else which keeps him in power.

Through the years, the Filipino people have steadily lost their sovereignty to U.S. imperialism, especially during the Marcos regime, which has mortgaged future generations of Filipinos to the IMF-WB. The martial law regime provided the U.S. government with unhampered use of the bases, provided terrific incentives to U.S. TNCs, allowed the exploitation of our resources and labor, and provided U.S. businesses with a huge market for their products. By using him as their puppet, the U.S. had kept Marcos in power. The U.S.-Marcos dictatorship flourished, but not our economy, not our country, not the Filipino people. Despite human rights violations and the loss of the people's liberties in the Philippines, the U.S. has to support Marcos because he is its man.

The U.S. has no choice. Marcos is its guarantee to safeguard U.S. interests here. As Teodoro Locsin has written in *Mr. and Ms.,* the U.S. couldn't care less what happens in the election, so long as there is an election, no matter how dirty. The regime has to be legitimized worldwide, and the one sure way to do that is by announcing to the world that an election took place—a "sure sign that democracy is alive and well." It's the same story as the March 24 election in El Salvador. The dictators will continue holding onto their thrones as long as they still serve the purposes of their colonial master. They will be thrown out only if the U.S. finds an alternative, or if the people themselves do it. In either case, the U.S. is the loser, especially in the latter case. Resentment of the people against U.S. support for Marcos will deepen and anti-American expressions will escalate.

You would think Washington would have learned from its mistakes. But no, the same game will continue to be played despite Cuba, Vietnam, Iran, Nicaragua. There will always be blatant U.S. interference in the sovereignty of small Third World countries and, in its vindictiveness, it will wage covert military and economic wars against those who would want to free themselves from the eagle's claws. Beirut, Grenada, and the borders of Nicaragua, where the contras are waging a desperate war against the people, are the latest battlegrounds. How many more years before the Philippines becomes the battleground?

A number of you are Americans, and it is difficult to approximate the pain in your heart when there is talk of U.S. imperialism, especially for those of you who take it personally. I would like to believe that I understand why some would be threatened by this kind of talk and would equate our nationalism with anti-Americanism. But sooner or later you have to accept this truth. Read through the pages of Penny Lernoux's *Cry of the People,* and if her book does not convince you of the evil of U.S. imperialism, I don't know what will. Transpose those realities into realities here and you have a perfect parallel. Only the names of places, rulers, and victims change. Otherwise, there is just one story.

Attorney Pepe Diokno has time and again defined his anti-American stance in the perspective of his nationalist orientation. He speaks for the hundreds among our people who, through the years, have understood the structural basis of U.S. imperialism. He has been forceful and eloquent in defining this stance: no to U.S. interference and the loss of our sovereignty; dismantle the U.S. military bases, for their presence leads to interference; no to the nuclear plant and storage of nuclear weapons; discipline the TNCs and do not allow them to operate without restrictions, etc.

To take this stand is not to be against the American people. The outrage is directed at American institutions, government, military, banks, businesses, and the like that have no compassion for the poor and needy. Those institutions are motivated by the contemporary idols of power, wealth, and influence. In their idolatry they have destroyed millions of people and will continue to devour helpless and powerless victims. In their attempt to maintain America's influence and to guarantee high living standards for the middle and upper classes in the U.S., those institutions have supported dictatorships, set up banana republics, plundered the resources of small countries, waged wars against liberation movements, dumped their products on Third World markets, and provided loans which ultimately revert to their own benefit. The U.S. is rich because so many small countries are poor.

But the American people, since they are supposedly the ones who elect their leaders, are collectively accountable for the conduct of such institutions. The question is, How much control do the Americans, especially those among the grass-roots and working class, have over their government? How much control does their government have over the banking and business institutions? What percentage of Americans actually and objectively understand the basic framework of U.S. imperialism? For all their rhetoric about a legacy of democracy and their forefathers fighting a war of justice and freedom for all, their memory has proved to be short. Now that many people in Third World countries are fighting their own wars for justice and freedom, they see the U.S. siding with their oppressors who care little about democracy except for empty rhetoric about it.

The other reality is that there are thousands of Americans who do understand the structural perspective and want to help dismantle U.S. imperialism. They see the contradictions within their own society and know that there is a sector at the bottom that is also composed of victims: the blacks, the urban poor, the unemployed, single mothers, and immigrants. They either belong to that sector or have opted to take the side of the marginalized. They know how it is to be poor and powerless, so they can relate with their counterparts in the Third World. In their hearts they know that these struggles are interconnected, and that the struggles must be intertwined.

Pablo Neruda, the Nobel Prize winner and Chile's most renowned poet, wrote in his memoirs: "I was touched by the echo my poems, violently anti-imperialist, stirred up in that North American crowd. I understood many things there, in Washington and California, where students and ordinary people showed approval of my works against imperialism. I learned on the spot that the North American enemies of our people were also enemies of the North American people." This reality brings to the fore the need for building bridges and dismantling the high walls that block our reaching out to each other in solidarity.

A CALL FOR NATIONAL RECONCILIATION

Karl notes that Aquino's decision to return to the Philippines was made in the context of a call for national reconciliation issued from various quarters.

[Aug. 25, 1983] The bishops declared on August 14 a National Day for Prayer and Reconciliation and called on the faithful "to offer reparation to the Lord for all violations of human rights committed by the right and the left." The weekend before this, the Concerned Lawyers Union of Mindanao held its convention in Davao City and their keynote speaker, the nationalist historian Renato Constantino, spoke on human rights. He was quoted as saying: "If we look more closely at the human rights situation, we will see that behind every human rights violation is a neocolonial policy or program aimed at entrenching the role of external forces in the country. . . . For when a big power controls a small nation economically and imposes its political and military influence to the point where the latter loses her right to determine her own goals for the welfare of her people, human rights are violated on a mass scale."

[Sept. 8, 1983] For some time now, all the major institutions have been calling for national reconciliation. The government through its controlled media has been pushing this line, attempting to win the hearts and minds of the citizenry. By declaring 1984 as the Jubilee Year for Penance and Reconciliation, the bishops have exhorted the faithful to work for unity and reconciliation. The private sector, through various organizations, has backed up the call. It was within this perspective that Aquino came home. Ironically, his death may have further driven a wedge between the rulers and the people, thus rendering reconciliation even less possible.

There are those who believe that Aquino is the sacrificial lamb that will facilitate the reconciliation process. On the other hand, there are also many people who subscribe to the belief that unless there is a structural transformation there can never be genuine national reconciliation. It is easy enough for those at the top of the pyramidal structure of society to call for reconciliation. One can be cynical and say that those at the top want the poor and oppressed majority to reconcile themselves to the interests, priorities, and schemes of the elite. Have they asked the people what should be initiated first so that steps can be taken towards genuine reconciliation, or have they again imposed their own strategies which more and more of the masses reject?

There can never be national reconciliation while the U.S. interests, IMF-WB loans, military bases, and TNCs protected by the puppet government continue to dominate us. No reconciliation can occur as long as the country's land and wealth are in the hands of a privileged few who continue to accumulate more wealth as well as to hold onto powerful political positions. A state characterized by graft and corruption, by unlimited generosity to relatives and cronies, by an extravagant display of wealth and capricious spending, and by a twisted sense of priorities cannot be in a position to lead the people towards reconciliation. As long as there are political prisoners, genuine reconciliation is a myth!

The people will say yes to reconciliation, but they know full well that it takes more than slogans and sincere intentions to effect this in our present society. We must address ourselves to the root cause of our people's impoverishment and marginalization. Democracy cannot be the privilege of only those in power but must be a living reality for all. Justice must reign supreme; truth be allowed its rightful place in the arena of knowledge and information. Political prisoners must all be released. The privilege of the writ of *habeas corpus* must be restored.

The dream of a society reconciled because there is justice and peace will be fulfilled one day. It will not come because those who hold power decide that it is our society's priority. It will be realized because the politicized poor will work, struggle, and die for it. It will not come from empty words and illusory promises but from the bitter sweat and precious blood of the heroes and martyrs, the great majority of whom will be from the ranks of the lowly and downtrodden. This scenario of the future and our belief in God's mercy make us cling to this hope. Our "faith gives substance to our hope and makes us certain of realities we do not see" (Heb. 11:1).

THE ELECTION, MAY 1984

In the May elections of 1984, opposition groups in the Philippines split. Some opted for participation, believing that they could effect some change from within the National Assembly. Others opted to boycott, believing the election to be a farce.

[April 7, 1984] The tumultuous days that have followed the death [Aquino's] on the tarmac have revealed the intensity of the people's anger and manifested the extent of their dissent. Even the most passive, privileged sectors have taken to the streets to clamor for the ousting of the U.S.-Marcos dictatorship. This May 14 election circus has been promoted in an attempt to diffuse dissent by dividing the opposition. True enough, the opposition crumbled with opportunists and short-sighted activists opting to be part of the farce. Fortunately, the boycott movement has persisted, expressing the need for a radical option. In the process, the authentic opposition, composed of men and women of proven integrity, has surfaced with a burning nationalist fervor to reclaim the people's sovereignty.

For many of us, opting for boycott is a moral imperative. It is an act of conscience not to provide legitimacy to this farce. To denounce the election as contrary to the people's dignity is a prophetic act demanded by the gospel because the people have a right to lay down the conditions for a meaningful election.

[May 23, 1984] It is a season to fast as an expression of our alignment with the politicized poor and the militant sectors of our society in their opinion to boycott the May 14 farcical elections. A week before the elections, a *Lakbayan* march was to converge on Davao City, coming from the north and the south. Thousands of peasants, workers, students, and people from other sectors were expected to join the thirty-kilometer march. We decided to express our solidarity with those who participated in the two-day march by fasting.

Since this fast occurred at a time when we were still waiting for Col. Valderama to dialogue with us, we made it known that we were fasting in solidarity with the *Lakbayan* marchers rather than to pressure him. But, because of the media coverage of our fast and of our request for a dialogue, he got angry. In time we were able to convince him that our fast transcended our "smaller concerns," since the fast was to express once again the call for general amnesty and the release of all political detainees which has been championed by the boycott movement. Two days after we broke our fast, our relatives and friends also went on a one-day fast in response to the same call.

The elections came and went. The imperialist forces and the CIA won once again! Of course the establishment media declared it "a triumph of democracy," words that would feed the news stories emanating from Washington. There was supposedly a heavy turn-out of voters, thus defeating the boycotters. However, those who truly understand the heavy demands of a radical transformation of society know in their hearts that the boycott was not a lost cause. If 5 percent of the voters boycotted, it would have been quite significant. It is less important to be successful than to be faithful to the call to continue the struggle.

REFLECTIONS ON NATIONAL HEROES' DAY

The anniversary of the death of Andres Bonifacio, a hero of the Philippine Revolution of 1898, prompted reflections on the meaning of National Heroes Day in the context of 1983:

[Nov. 30, 1983] Today we celebrate National Heroes Day and remember the Filipino patriot who continues to inspire the people to liberate themselves from foreign domination and oppression—Andres Bonifacio. As I woke up, someone sang Bonifacio's song, "Love for one's land of birth." The song echoed through the cells during the whole day, reminding us of last year's hunger strike when we adopted this as our theme song.

A fast for life and freedom was to start today among the detainees of the various detention centers in Metro Manila and their relatives and supporters. When we first heard of this plan, we considered joining the Manila detainees as an act of solidarity. After all, the main demands of the fast, the declaration of a general amnesty and the release of all detainees, if granted, would benefit all political prisoners. Our sympathy fast was to be a way of expressing our own anguish over the present repressive situation and our cry for justice.

For a week we went through a reflection and consultation process to determine whether we would go on this sympathy fast or not. Pros and cons were brought up and discussed. After the consultation, we decided that we would not join. Our relatives, in fact, did not encourage us, saying that this time they would be doing the fasting themselves.

Today is a public holiday, so we had no sunning and no visitors. We stayed padlocked in our cells with our quiet thoughts on how to be a hero in our society that demands the emergence of genuine heroes who are anchored in the struggle of the toiling masses. There have always been and always will be heroes in our midst, whether it be during the 1890s when Filipinos fought a revolution to free the country from the Spanish tyrants, or in the present when our people are freeing themselves from the shackles of an oppressive dictatorship. As the heroine in the novel *Burger's Daughter* said: "There will always be those who cannot live with themselves at the expense of the fullness of life of others."

Of course the regime will have its own celebrations today with hollow speeches and crocodile tears. Ironically, it is the very same regime whose brutality has triggered off the patriotism of the present-day heroes. The going was very rough in the early years of martial law, when the great majority was paralyzed by fear and fed by controlled media about how happy the people were with the "new society." With the ever-worsening economic crisis and escalating militarization on the one hand, and the growing militancy of the politicized sectors on the other hand, dissent has become widespread and more people are willing to take the risks that come with a radical commitment.

REFLECTION ON THE THIRTY-SEVENTH COMMEMORATION OF PHILIPPINE INDEPENDENCE DAY

[June 8, 1984] Four days from now, we celebrate Independence Day. It will also be the start of the Muslim *Ramadhan*.

It is very ironic that our dictatorial government will make a big show of this Independence Day, as they have done in the past years. But the irony is not lost among more and more people. There can never be a genuine Independence Day celebration as long as there are political detainees. The blood shed by the heroes of the 1890s that led to the event of June 12, 1898, has not yet led to the birth of a truly free and independent nation. More blood is being shed and will still flow before peace and freedom will reign.

We are going to celebrate this day with a fast.

INTERNATIONAL SCENE

Karl's interest in history goes beyond the confines of the national situation.

[Aug. 25, 1983] Despite being cut off from the rest of the world, I can't help but be overwhelmed by the continuing flow of events in the past weeks both here and elsewhere. We have much time to listen to radio news and read daily newspapers and weekly news magazines, courtesy of kind friends, as well as to reflect on the implications of the events reported, and we are perhaps more affected by them.

Prison life also provides time to situate events within a broader context which can provoke new dimensions of anger and anxiety. Definitely, we have leisure to read between the lines and surmise the part of the news that remains unreported. We are perhaps in a better position to see how events are inextricably linked. This is one "blessing" of serving time behind bars.

As we ended our hunger strike, news came about the hundreds of political prisoners in Turkey who went on a mass hunger strike to protest their harsh prison conditions. It was frustrating not to get details of the result of their fast. We could only hope they had some success, as we did, no matter how small. Then recently, there was report about the group of four, including one couple, in Oakland who shared their "International Fast for Life" with people in other countries. They have been fasting to protest the nuclear build-up of the superpowers, and they intend to abstain until some immediate and significant steps towards peace are taken. The anniversary of the bombing of Hiroshima was just recently celebrated amidst worldwide fear of a nuclear war. "It is a sin to build a nuclear weapon!" is the shout coming from modern-day prophets, but those who hold the world captive by their power and might refuse to listen. And our own ex-Senator Lorenzo Tañada declares that we are losing the battle against the setting up of the Bataan Nuclear Power Plant in our own land.

Poland just recently lifted its martial law, and hundreds of political prisoners were reportedly provided amnesty and released. Like the lifting of martial law in the Philippines, there are reports that the gesture was a farce, undertaken for cosmetic purposes. The church played a major role in the lifting, given the pope's recent visit to his homeland. President Marcos has lifted the Presidential Commitment Order (PCO), but so far no political detainee has been provided amnesty. In fact only the name has been changed, for the president decreed that he continues to hold the right for a Preventive Detention Action (PDA), basically no different from PCO. The president announced the abolition of the PCO the day before the bishop's pastoral letter calling the PCO "immoral" was to be read in churches nationwide. . . .

The wildfire of communal ethnic violence that has raged across Sri Lanka following another tense breakdown in Sinhala-Tamil relations was undoubtedly the main event in Asia recently. The unprecedented orgy of racial violence led to the massacre of Tamils in prison, in their homes, and on the streets. In 1979 during the Asian Theological Conference held in Sri Lanka, I was part of a group that went on exposure to the north to look into this issue. Even at that time the tension could already be felt, and we knew it would only be a few years before it would explode. The report of the *Far Eastern Economic Review* mentioned that Sri Lanka's papal nuncio was asked to leave the country because of "his contacts in Jaffna, where some members of the Roman Catholic Clergy are supporters of the separatist movement." The same week that these events were happening in that paradise island, the church on the island of Mindanao faced another round of persecution. A diocesan priest in the diocese of Tandag, Surigao del Sur, and a lay leader were arrested and later charged with sedition and inciting to rebellion. Coaccused are two other priests, two nuns, and two lay leaders who were being hunted by the military. A few days later a convent in the diocese of Iligan in Lanao del Norte was raided, and the parish priest would have been arrested except that he was out of town. Another convent was ransacked and the robbers took away the materials used for conscientization. A church worker involved in the labor program of the diocese who "disappeared" two months ago remains missing. . . .

The frustrating part about all this, especially for us detainees, is the helplessness of not being able to do something to respond to some of those problems. We can only pray and encourage friends who are concerned.

THE CASSANDRA TRAGEDY

[Nov. 27, 1983] The shock of the day was when we heard the news about the sea tragedy off Surigao. Early in the week the M/V Cassandra, on its way to Cebu, got hit by a typhoon and sank in the deep sea. We learned earlier that among the seven religious women who perished were four who used to come and visit us regularly, including Sister Catherine, R.G.S., who was with the TFDP–Davao and became a good friend of the detainees. We were optimistic at first since the news from the local media claimed very few fatalities. However, this morning we were told that the greater probability was that Sisters Consuelo, Catherine, Concepción, and Jo perished with the boat.

As if this were not shocking enough, we were informed that there were other friends on the boat, and there was no hope that their bodies could be recovered. A Carmelite priest, three other religious women, and four lay workers also perished in the same sea tragedy. Since most of them were close friends, I felt a tremendous sense of loss. All through the day I kept on asking: "Why, Lord? Why them?" There are so many other priests, nuns, and lay workers who are not involved in building a just society where kingdom-values flourish. Why take away the few who are trying their best to be faithful to the call of the gospel? What are you trying to tell us?

In theory it is easy to acknowledge that God's ways are strange. But when God's ways bring pain and grief, it is hard to accept. The comforting thought, of course, is our belief in the resurrection, but this can seem so abstract. Perhaps a more concrete source of comfort is the thought that those who died have left us a legacy. Up to the end of their lives they were consistent in their commitment to serve other people. A few survivors claimed that they last saw the nuns helping to save other people, especially the children. At the threshold of death, they remained faithful to the call of service!

[Dec. 4, 1983] Tears flowed during the memorial mass for the Cassandra victims this morning. A big crowd of relatives and friends came to join us in paying tribute to the sisters and lay workers who perished.

The liturgical celebration was meant to convey our joy and hope in the resurrection. In fact, we had brought our Christmas decorations to provide color to the surroundings. While we did reflect on the meaning of the resurrection in the lives of those who serve the people, we couldn't help but feel the pain of the tragic parting. Besides, as one sister said, the sorrow is far more intense because there are no bodies to mourn. They are lost forever in the sea.

The detainees offered their tribute in songs, poems, and personal testimonies to the memory of the four sisters who have been part of our lives here. A few recalled how Sisters Consuelo, Catherine, Jo, and Concepción touched their lives, offered them comfort, and provided them hope and encouragement. Tears fell as we sang the song that Sister Catherine had encouraged us to submit to the TFDP songwriting contest.

It was, however, the testimony of Betty's father-in-law, whose two sons the military claim are with the NPA in the hills, that really caused the flood of tears.

Mr. de Vera, about eighty and looking like everyone's favorite grandfather, spoke straight from his heart: "If it was possible to exchange my life with those of the sisters, I would gladly do so. I am already an old man and there's very little I can do for other people in need. The sisters were young and they could still do a lot of service. Why doesn't God take me, and bring the sisters back?"

Father Louie Hechanova, C.SS.R., from AMRSP, concelebrated the Mass, and he told us of the memorial celebration to be held in Manila the next week. He was going to take our statement and poems to be read at that celebration. The memorial Mass took almost two hours. Fortunately the guards were considerate and didn't cut it short. However, as soon as the Mass ended, we were padlocked. Like a typical rural funeral celebration, however, the event included a shared meal as we feasted on the *arroz caldo* and *lanzones* brought by the relatives and friends. . . .

CONCLUSION

[March 25, 1984] All of us will have our own date with history. The luckier ones will live to see history fulfill the promise of our forefathers' dream. The nobler ones will have found their rest, even as their legacy contributes to a people's outrage and dissent. Every time a martyr falls victim to the regime's brutality, the blood he or she sheds is the red ink that records a life-giving sacrifice. The tribute may not be paid now, but one day a grateful nation will remember and will sing songs in memory of its heroes. May we live to see that day!

This history, however, is integrated into the totality of salvation history. The Lord of history reigns across time and space. This is the very same Lord who liberated the people of God from the cruel Pharaoh, the oppressive conquerors, the despotic rulers, the repressive kings, and the fascist dictators. God has brought the people into an awareness of their dignity; God has challenged them to rise up to struggle for their rights and has guided them through their mass actions toward deliverance from captivity. God will lead them to a land where there are no inequalities and injustices, to a land where the people will not go hungry and will not be tortured by the army of their rulers. Here the promise of the kingdom has a chance to be fulfilled.

Our faith has to be anchored in the eventuality of the kingdom's fulfillment. The expression of our faith has to be related to this salvation history. The concrete manner of expressing this faith has to be contextualized in the people's struggle for liberation. We have to get involved in serving the people, no matter how high the cost of discipleship or the risks involved.

To have spent one year in prison is so little compared to what others have offered to keep alive the people's dream, the hopes, tears, defeats, temporary victories, and continuing struggles.

P.S. It is early morning of March 26, 1984, the anniversary of my arrest. As I drowsily get into bed, I pray that I will not be here on March 26, 1985. Can such an anniversary be happy? Not happy perhaps, but certainly meaningful. Cheers!

4

Discipleship Viewed through Barbed Wire

A Christian who, for fear of suffering and death, refuses to be at the heart of the struggle to forge a just and righteous society that foreshadows the kingdom of peace and love has never understood the life-giving message of the resurrection. We find life—the life that matters—by offering ourselves in the struggle.

K. Gaspar

THE COST OF DISCIPLESHIP

Discipleship and its meaning for the committed Christian in today's context is a central theme for Karl. Time and again he returns to this theme in his writings. In a series of reflections on discipleship written a month after the beginning of a fast and hunger strike which was to last forty-four days, he asks:

Is it inevitable that sooner or later a follower is confronted with the cross which spells out the price of dicipleship? Can one be rich, privileged, and powerful and at the same time claim to take the gospel seriously? Or are only the poor, deprived, and powerless ready to receive the seed of the word of God?

For Karl the answer is clear. In a letter to the Maryknoll Sisters for their 1984 regional assembly, he writes:

There is no question but that we have to strive to incarnate the gospel in our contemporary societal context. But we must also incarnate ourselves into the context addressed by the gospel today, a context which is dominated by poverty, deprivation, and marginalization. We are challenged to genuinely take a preferential option for the poor, to truly understand the cry of the deprived to reclaim their lost dignity, and to immerse ourselves in the struggle of the marginalized for the freedom to chart their own destiny. These are big words that could easily be just clichés or slogans full of fire and fury but devoid of praxis. But I trust that as women of wisdom and vision you are finding and certainly will find ways to put flesh on these words.

Teilhard de Chardin has said that "love requires us not only to bind up wounds but to be in the first ranks of the movement to change society." This thought can give us a further perspective on our attempt to be true to the gospel. We cannot just be concerned with healing persons; our concern must be to heal a sick society suffering from a malignant tumor which is evident in the inequitable distribution of wealth. We must concern ourselves with the diagnosis of this sick society. We cannot content ourselves with playing nurse to people with broken arms or hearts but must strive to be one of those who have gone through life with broken dreams. With them we have to learn how to dream of a just society and how to pay the price to make that dream come true for future generations. If we are with Jesus, as he moves through the crowds healing the sick and offering comfort, we must go with him all the way. His death on the cross was the sign of his willingness to confront the powers of his own day. To be with him today is to walk the same path. It is only in daring to challenge the validity and legitimacy of a dehumanizing, established order—even, if need be, at the cost of one's own life—that we can claim to be his follower.

In societies where the extent of dehumanization has assumed such proportions that the cry for justice reaches the heavens and in a land where God's people are subjected to the brutal repercussions of impoverishment and repression, discipleship commits the follower to action on behalf of justice as an essential element of preaching the gospel.

In a country where the doctrine of national security serves as an umbrella justifying the military's acts of violence against its own people, the disciples who take the gospel seriously are placed in a rather risky position. They feed the hungry but get into trouble if they give food to suspected dissidents. They shelter the homeless refugees but are abused by the military for aiding "sympathizers of the rebels." They visit political prisoners and are marked as friends of subversives. They champion the cause of widows and orphans whose husbands and fathers are summarily executed by government troops, and soon they have a dossier in the military camp to be used against them once they are arrested. They denounce the continuing violation of human rights, and could be charged in court for inciting to rebellion. To top it all, they are themselves labeled communists!

. . . It is very easy for disciples to be intimidated by the powers-that-be and to give in to the temptation to allow their commitment to become merely spiritual. They will engage in safe ministries which do not place them on a collision course with the establishment, and they will avoid any involvement that might demand a prophetic stance. They will react strongly against those who would make an option for the biblical call to justice and love on the pretext that such an option might be open to the charge of following Marx rather than Christ.

Karl reflects upon the cost of discipleship in a letter to Jim Wallis:

[Aug. 30, 1984] You are out of prison now but you'll be back. I am still in but if they release me tomorrow I may be back the following day. We are men marked by the options we have taken, each in his own historical context. I pray that we will not succumb to the temptation evoked by fear and lack of belief in God's saving grace. May we, instead, continue to risk our necks and, with all those on the same journey, hold on with faith and courage.

The most urgent thing to do is to get rid of fear, to undergo a Pentecost, to muster the courage to stand up to the risks and to become convinced that there is nothing to fear but fear itself. Like the apostles of old, the disciples of today have to give up the safety of hiding behind closed doors in order to face the responsibility that a radical witnessing to Christ demands and to embrace the inevitable consequences of such a militant conversion. Once they manage to liberate themselves from the paralyzing effects of fear then a breakthrough will have been made. We know that Christ himself had to overcome the fear which struck him intensely in the Garden of Gethsemane before he was able to prepare himself for the pain and tragedy of Good Friday. Mary, his mother, must have known fear from the very start. Fear prevented Jesus' best friends from sharing his last moments on Calvary. Fear made Peter lie. Paul, too, must have experienced the raw intensity of fear in his travels as he encountered shipwreck, storms, and prison life.

We no longer have to look back to the early life of the church when disciples were stoned to death or to the various stages of church persecution when Christians were martyred for their faith in order to put flesh to the words of Christ that "the servant will be no greater than the master." The disciples of Jesus continued to be harassed. The followers are still persecuted. Martyrs around the globe today continue giving their lives for their friends. The community of faith still experiences the arrest, detention, and even massacre of some of its members.

The warnings of Mark 13:9–13 and Matthew 10:16–25 are with us even today. The cost of discipleship is high. Men and women are confronted with a life and death struggle within our midst, in our own times. Some of our own friends, relatives, coworkers, and other kindred spirits are both the victims and the offerings. They are not faceless people out there in some isolated area like Russia or El Salvador. They are our very own loved ones whose passion and suffering jolt us into the realization that what we had feared in the past has now become a tragic reality in the present.

"Why me, Lord?" disciples ask. "Is it worth the pain and the sleepless nights?" The temptation to give up everything and to succumb to the impact of fear is so great. . . . It is only by the grace of God, the support and solidarity of relatives and friends, and the deepening conviction of the disciples that they must hold onto their role in the urgent task of social transformation that can save them from fear and from the sense of fatalism that makes them want to give up what they have begun.

TO THE NEGROS NINE

[February 11, 1984—on the Negros Nine see also pp. 26–29 and 139–141] I am sure that all of you have come face to face with the same question: "Why me, Lord?" It is a question that we no longer ask ourselves individually but collectively. "Why are these things happening to us, Lord? Why are a growing number of our people being harassed, arrested, tortured, and salvaged? Why are church-workers faced with persecution which seems to be so inevitable in Third World countries today?"

Persecution is to be expected whenever an option is taken to denounce injustice and to announce the kingdom of truth and freedom. You are manifesting a discipleship rooted in justice. Those who stand to lose much power and wealth upon the inauguration of a just society tremble at this form of witnessing. They will not allow you to continue disturbing the "peace and order" which is so essential to the established order they want to keep intact.

Father Jon Sobrino, the Jesuit theologian from El Salvador, wrote that "persecution comes precisely when the church goes out of itself, ceases to defend its own rights, and turns outward to defend the rights of the people." You are not on trial because of murder, illegal possession of arms, and subversion—although these are the formal charges against you. You are on trial because you dared to defend the rights of the people against the abuses of those who have usurped the people's sovereignity! You have become an enemy of the state precisely because you have sought to support the people's struggle to assert their God-given dignity and not be cowed into subservience like the slaves of Pharaoh's day.

. . . The light these days seems to come from the expanding protest movement both in the cities and in the countryside. Will it succeed in mobilizing the mass movements and the opposition toward democratization and full restoration of the people's rights? Cut off as we are in prison from that dynamism, all we can do is pray that there will be a breakthrough in the struggle for a radical change through the militant march of the many.

Meanwhile we reach out to encourage each other in our common plight. Like those sturdy eucalyptus trees that dominate the plains of Perth, we have the strength to stand firm in our witness to Jesus and the grace to sway with the Spirit's challenge to build the kingdom.

I end this letter with a reflection by an expolitical detainee, a lay churchworker who like you was arrested because of a commitment to the gospel. Her words may bring you comfort as you wait for your release from captivity:

> As long as I can see
> a bit of sky, a bit of blue
> beyond the wires, beyond the bars,
> I know I can be true
> and dare to dream
> and dare to fight
> and dare to pay the price
> of freedom longed for
> justice sought
> and truth
> for land beloved.

> *Leonore Sevilla*
> *—detained in Davao, Jan. 16, 1982*

RISKS OF LAY CHURCH WORKERS

[March 1984] If the trend does not drastically change in the next few years, lay church workers will probably become one of our endangered species! This might be a rather overly dramatic statement, but there is need to underscore this tragic reality of the risks being taken by layworkers in Mindanao today. I say this loudly and clearly to impress upon us the dangers that come with our work so that we no longer hold onto any illusion that we are less vulnerable just because we have some form of protection. Besides, to be forewarned is to be forearmed.

The present situation in Mindanao has reached a level of violence unprecedented in our region's history—a violence perpetuated by the regime in order to maintain itself in power. Knowing full well that it has become extremely isolated from the people—and apart from hoping to win their hearts and minds—the repressive regime has resorted to a strategy that reveals its desperate effort to maintain its dominant position. This strategy is to crush the people's dissent at all cost, to quell the social unrest no matter how brutal the means employed, and to force the people to remain subservient to its power despite its immoral character.

The result has been devastating and deadly. Thousands have been uprooted from farms and homes. Communities have been subjected to the atrocities that more often than not are part of military operations. Picket lines have been forcefully disbanded and labor leaders shot. Farm-leaders disappear in the night and are later claimed dead by their widows. Ordinary citizens have been salvaged, and later the papers reported they were terrorists killed during encounters. Hundreds have been arrested, tortured, and detained indefinitely in congested prison cells. The list of atrocities continues to accumulate names of more victims *ad nauseam.*

No one can claim to be safe with this kind of violence being inflicted on our people across the bleeding land. Not one sector has been spared the agony and death that are trademarks of a fascist regime. Peasants, tribal communities, workers, industrial laborers, women, the urban poor, students, and professionals have fallen victims to the tragedy of our times. Among these sectors is that of churchworkers, including priests, religious, catechists, lay leaders, and justice and peace workers. From Agusan to Iligan, from Davao to Zamboanga, they have accumulated in number. Chances are the number will increase as more commit themselves to follow Christ's example of giving up one's life for the sake of the poor and oppressed.

But the people are far more courageous in the face of death. They have become stronger in their just claim for a place in a society that respects their dignity. They have joined with a passion only the oppressed can muster in the struggle for justice, freedom, and democracy. The awakening and ensuing commitment of the people to fight for liberation is the good news for all of us today.

On our part we should realize that to take God's creation and redemption seriously and not fight all forces of injustice and death is an impossibility, a flat contradiction of the Gospel. We should carry on the task of accompanying our people in their *Lakbayan* toward a just society.

May we all continue to have the prophetic courage of the just! May we all be faithful to the challenge of serving the people. And may our solidarity with one another be anchored in the hope that one day we shall overcome!

COURAGE AND COMMITMENT

A young man who was a cellmate of Karl's left a deep impression on him. In his Christmas reflections Karl writes movingly of the courage and commitment of this eighteen-year-old companion.

[Christmas 1983] At one time I shared a cell with six other detainees. The youngest, Godoy, an eighteen-year-old boy, was the most impressive, and his commitment to serve the people has humbled me. His bed was beside mine, so there were nights when, talking in whispers, I listened to him share his awakening and involvement in the struggle. When I first met him, I noticed a big scar across his chest. He told me that it was a remembrance of the days when he thought he would be salvaged. But the military kept him alive after almost a week of endless torture.

He was ready to die when he was arrested. He had friends who had disappeared. He knew that if he got caught, his chances of being salvaged were high. Without any hesitation or shallow modesty, he said he was ready to die for his commitment. When he got involved, it was taken for granted that some would get killed because of their involvement. He had accepted the fact that he could be one of those who would die in the service of his country. So when he was picked up, he accepted the high probability of death.

Of course he is thankful for the fact that he is still alive. But he keeps on saying that he will die before reaching thirty. He knows what he will do if he ever gets released. There is no turning back. One has to be ready to offer one's life in the service of the people. He says it without batting an eyelash and I know he really means it. His favorite song (all sung in whispers) is the one about shedding one's blood so that the country will be free.

He is so young and yet so mature in his outlook on life. He is part of this country's youth who have given up on their elders' inability to build a just society and now accept the challenge to fashion a new destiny for themselves and the generations that will follow them. I am embarrassed at how naive and apolitical I was in my early years. Even now the intensity and strength of this boy's commitment is beyond me. I do not have his courage to be ready to face the ultimate price of service to one's brothers and sisters.

[April 1984] You remember Godoy, the eighteen-year-old boy I wrote about in my Christmas reflections? Two weeks ago he was released on bail after his PCO was lifted. At the end of this month he would have spent a year in prison. We were of course overjoyed by his release, but we miss him. He is especially missed by his buddy Terio, who is going through a depression again. Just a week before Godoy was released, his cousin Tony, who has the same effervescence and disproves that line which says "youth is wasted on the young," was padlocked here.

Tony was arrested along with two girls and another young man in early March, but they were detained first in a nearby town before being brought here a month later. One of the girls was raped, and all four were tortured. When they got here the torture wounds had healed, but the marks remain clear on their scarred bodies. Poor kids, though so young and fragile they are already battered. However, they are unbelievably strong and firm in their commitment.

THEY BEAR CHRIST'S PAIN IN THEIR BODIES

[June 1983] The center of discipleship is Jesus. The core event of Jesus' life is his death and resurrection. Disciples cease to be faithful followers if they veer away from the footsteps of Jesus, the footsteps that reached Gethsemane and Golgotha. If they do not accept the inevitability of the cross and are not ready to embrace it when it comes their way, disciples are just like the young man who "went away sorrowful" (Mark 10:22).

Still Another Detainee Salvaged

we heard he was padlocked
all by himself
in the *bartolina*
on a sunday.

we didn't know who he was,
where he came from,
why he was arrested,
and on what day.

we all knew intuitively
that he needed urgent help;
there could be further torture
if there was delay.

we couldn't do anything else
but pass the word outside,
help! send a lawyer!
ahora mismo! today!

sunday and monday passed;
no relatives or lawyer came,
but he was finally surfaced
on the third day.

he was brought out in the sun
a figure straight from *el greco,*
gaunt, thin, with soulful eyes,
half-dead, that tuesday.

we embraced him with our eyes,
saw the wound on the forehead;
blood was still oozing out.
then, they took him away.

again, the bastards took him away.
haven't they extracted everything
from him? so why go on?
he's practically dead anyway.

like lazarus he came out of the tomb,
but in the light, there wasn't
much promise of joy
for us, that tuesday.

wednesday, thursday passed.
we didn't see him any longer.
we wanted to know where he was,
but there was no way.

friday night, word came in a whisper:
he is no longer in prison.
at 2:00 o'clock that afternoon
they had taken him to a place far away.

is he alive? or is he dead?
no one among us knows.
since he disappeared, we can't
do anything but pray.

(A day after I wrote this poem
word came that a detainee saw his
dead body inside a *fiera*.)

TORTURE

[Feb. 1984] Torture is inflicted on practically everyone arrested so that after a while one becomes numb and no longer has enough interest even to ask new detainees what torture techniques were used on them. . . .

The manner, the setting, and the perpetrators of torture vary from one experience to another. Name any torture technique, from the electric shock treatment to the water cure, and chances are it has been used on a detainee here. The setting ranges from a local outpost to an isolated safehouse. Enlisted men, intelligence men, CHDF, and paramilitary subordinates all have blood on their hands. . . .

It is to the honor of the many who experience such harrowing ordeals that they survive with their dignity intact. When detainees do not submit themselves to the will of their torturers, they prove once again that while they may be dehumanized by the act of torture, nothing and no one can rob them of their dignity. The body may break down, but the will remains solid and firm. One experiences the pain but is more concerned with retaining the memory of a dream that refuses to die!

The scars of the bodily harm inflicted on some of the detainees remain to give witness to the brutality of militarism. I have a cell mate whose back is still broken two months after a soldier jumped on it at the height of the torture sessions. He limps around the cell and seems helpless. Across from us in the next cell is a young boy who is not himself. He stares endlessly out into a void where perhaps he finds escape. Word is that he was placed inside a drum which was rolled around while being hit on all sides.

TORTURE IN THE CONTEXT OF JESUS' PASSION

[May 1984] The disciple is no greater than the master. As Jesus went through torture in the process of expressing his willingness to redeem humanity so we too must be ready to go through such a dehumanizing experience as we join in the struggle for the liberation of our people.

The meek and mild image perpetuated by those who would reduce Christ to a weakling is contradicted by the dignity and serenity he revealed under pressure. The profile of the man who faced Pilate is one of profound inner strength. From him we gain confidence that we, too, can transcend our frailties and manage to show our captors that our spirits will not be broken just because they break our bodies.

But oftentimes the physical pain is so unbearable and the psychological pressure so great that the person being tortured breaks down and confesses. There are also cases in which the suffering becomes so intense that captives "confess" to the crimes being imputed to them or even make up stories just to end the torture session. . . .

Many detainees have gone through hell. Scars, physical or otherwise, remain and they are never the same again. What was done by the military to detainees in South Africa, Chile, South Korea, and other repressive countries, as documented by Amnesty International, bears testimony to the brutality of torture worldwide. However, it is a tribute to the human will that most detainees are able to survive and to show that the body may be broken but not the will to dream and to struggle.

DEATH

Frequently torture results in death. Karl writes in November 1983 concerning three young men who were salvaged.

The most dramatic feature of the day's activity was the funeral march for the three young men who were recently salvaged. Suspected of being subversives, they were summarily executed by the military and buried in a common, shallow grave in the municipal cemetary of Digos, sixty kilometers south of Davao City. The way the military brutally desecrated the bodies has caused outrage.

There was a meeting of the detainees' relatives yesterday along with the parents of the salvaged victims and the lawyers. The parents were going to Digos after the meeting to claim the bodies and take them to Davao City for the funeral march. However, they weren't sure whether they would be able to exhume the bodies as it is believed that the military is guarding the shallow grave for fear that relatives would exhume the bodies themselves. It reminds me of the Roman soldiers guarding the tomb where Jesus was buried. The rumor is that the military do not want the relatives to exhume the bodies because they had been burned! Such is the barbarity of those who are supposed to protect lives!

We tuned in on the radio the whole afternoon to find out whether the parents managed to claim their sons' bodies and how the march went. Unfortunately, no radio station covered the affair. So while our relatives and friends were out in the streets, we were in our cells making Christmas cards. All afternoon and evening we were kept in suspense even as we hoped that the parents succeeded in claiming their legitimate right—the last remains of their sons.

INNOCENT VICTIMS

As old detainees are released, new ones take their place. Two weeks ago, four new detainees, all young boys with an average age of eighteen years, were padlocked here. Their case is now in court, and they are charged with murder, sedition, and subversion. One look at the boys and the charges seem ludicrous. They look so fragile and innocent one cannot associate them with guns. The alleged leader of the group, Jimmy, wears a rosary around his neck and says that he is involved in the rosary crusade in his parish. They had been tortured mercilessly before they were brought here. A week after their arrest they appeared in court with their lawyers who demanded that they be transferred here for safety.

Yesterday—Ash Wednesday—our Lent was off to a gloomy

start. Just when we thought that the military's practice of *hulbot*—forcefully taking the detainees out for interrogation or to act as guides for military operations or even to be salvaged—had ceased because of our hunger strike, it happened again! The four, Jimmy, Lito, Jun, and his brother, Boy, were taken out and taken to another building in the compound. There they were blindfolded and interrogated and forced to confess. They were hit all over their fragile bodies by their interrogators. Jimmy received the heaviest beating. His head was covered with a plastic bag throughout the interrogation and torture, and he almost suffocated. The torture lasted from 1:00 P.M. until dusk, and when it was over they crept into our cells. They were pale and looked very frightened. Jimmy, haggard and forlorn, walked like a zombie down the aisle to their cell. One could feel the sense of outrage among the other prisoners whose collective heart reached out to these four victims of military abuse.

Just this morning the news report announced the death of another young man at the hands of the police. The night before he was picked up, interrogated, and tortured. In the morning he was released to an older sister who had been looking for him. She rushed him to the hospital where he died of internal hemorrhages.

So what else is new? The savagery of this fascist regime continues to devour innocent victims. There is outrage and an ever-deepening anger among those who are within the circle of victims. The wrath born of direct witnessing of such gross violations of human rights becomes part of the swelling dissent now escalating throughout the country. But placed against the backdrop of world events—the Iran-Iraq war, the Lebanon tragedies, the carnage in Central America, the current moves of the *apparatchik* in Moscow to send feelers to the other old man in Washington who is seeking re-election, etc.—local events pale in their "newsworthiness." But from the perspective of our cells, these are the events that matter much more, happening as they do right under our noses.

How long, Lord, before those in captivity are set free? How long before the night gives way to the new dawn so eagerly awaited but which seems to take forever to break out on the horizon? How many more bruised and dead bodies before the madness ends? How much more anger will explode across the wide plains of our bleeding land before a conflagration threatens to engulf us in a catastrophe?

Caught in a position of helplessness, the only thing we can do is look up to the heavens and cry out these questions, hoping that answers will soon come to bring relief. However, one knows the answers will not come easily precisely because these are born out of historical praxis. It is in the arena of the concrete reality of a prophetic struggle that we can hope to find the answers—no matter how tentative and vague—to these stirrings of the heart longing for peace.

Even though we in prison can only sit and wait, we hope that our collective stand puts us within the arena of the struggle, no matter how passive our role may be. We don't have too much to share in forging the answers to historical questions, but symbolically we might be able to challenge those who do. Now is definitely the season for such hopes. Who knows but that soon we just might go beyond being mere symbols and be in the midst of the actual work of building our common dream!

HOPE

[July 1984] Pain and grief are all over the land, and the immediate future does not promise a respite. In fact the long-term future does not point to a land of milk and honey unless there is drastic change in the social structures leading to a more equitable distribution of wealth and power. But this is unlikely. The detainees' suffering is but a piece of reality in the collage of a people's total situation of blood and tears. Their anxiety is but part of a scenario where death is common.

This is Christ's passion in the here and now, experienced by people oppressed by those who refuse to see the face of Christ among the lowly and downtrodden. Christ's pain is felt by those who are pushed to the bottom. His suffering is experienced by those who don't count in the arena of commerce and politics and whose rights as human beings are made dispensable by the dictates of "national security." His anxiety is in the hearts of mothers who intuitively know that their children will suffer the same wretched life and will never see the day when they can provide for them a better tomorrow.

Life shouldn't be experienced only as grief and anxiety but also as hope and joy. The Lord's death led to the resurrection. Our belief in God's justice as well as God's love for people convinces us that the people's suffering will lead to their liberation. In between, of course, is their struggle. As the struggle rages there is pain and grief. But the perspective is one of hope.

THE CHALLENGE TO LOVE

In prison there are a good number of fellow detainees who are definitely Good Samaritans. They are sensitive, considerate, and very helpful to those who need friendship and a listening ear. They provide a positive impact on the prison's tight atmosphere. Their generosity challenges others to share what they have. Their patience encourages others not to easily lose their temper, and their kindness extends to everyone, cell mates and guards alike. They live out the gospel message to be men and women for others.

LOVING THE ENEMY

Each detainee faces the question of loving the enemy and makes options accordingly. For some, it is easy enough to make the distinction between hating persons or hating the structure which breeds such persons. Others, however, who do not differentiate end up burning with hatred against the enemy and becoming vindictive. Among the guards there are one or two who have not been swallowed up by the corruption of brutality of the military complex and who still manage to act like gentlemen soldiers despite the pressures. The detainees respond to them with tremendous respect and appreciation. But the majority of the military have lost their humane traits, have surrendered all the goodness that might have been in their hearts, and have become willing tools of the state to oppress the detainees. It takes tremendous grace to accept them as fellow human beings as they have rejected the dignity of those under their supervision.

Love of enemy does not take place outside of a given concrete context. It is easy enough to claim the Christian virtue of being able to embrace an enemy if one speaks about fictional or imagined circumstances devoid of passion and raw emotions. The moment the issue is no longer in the abstract and involves concrete actions of human beings, forgiveness and reconciliation become very difficult. One admires the *Nicaragüenses* for having been able to forgive the *Somocistas* and prevent a bloodbath of attrition after the victory of the revolution in 1979. Influenced by Freire, there are those who say that love for the enemy can only be expressed in helping to liberate them as oppressors. This, of course, is done by the oppressed, as those in power will not voluntarily change since they are unconvinced that they have been dehumanized by their wealth and absolute power.

In a situation where a revolution is in progress, there are those who claim that love for the oppressed takes precedence over love for enemy. The latter is seen as a luxury. The enemies have to be eliminated, and this is justified because their continuing dominant position cannot allow the coming of the kingdom. The just-war theory provides the ethical guidelines. This is a very controversial area for Christians, and the division that separates those who opt for violence from those who would adhere to non-violence can create tremendous animosity.

Those who advocate nonviolence would place themselves in a vulnerable position in the hands of the enemy in order to break the enemy's hold over people. They believe that the moral force of their action has greater power than the brutal physical force of the enemy. Others see such a posture as too idealistic, even quixotic, an impossible dream of social transformation without the concomitant laying down of one's life in the context of a people's war. Each Christian, within his or her own conscience, has to resolve this conflict of options. Many go through a dark night of the soul attempting to crystallize their option and then live with it or even die for it. Ultimately, it is a covenant one makes with one's Creator in solidarity with those one is committed to serve.

THE CHALLENGE OF FASTING

The fast [see chap. 5] and hunger strike brought out the worst and the best from our fellow detainees and provided a rare and precious opportunity for manifesting concern for and solidarity with one another. Most of the detainees joined in.

The community experience of ours during the fast was but a reflection of what is happening in the broader Philippine society. There are more and more people now willing to take the risk and sacrifice their rights for the good of all.

But many still prefer to hold onto their little comforts and isolated safety. The fast provided us the time and space to show that we are concerned for each other's safety—and this alone made the hunger, the risks, and the anxiety worthwhile.

The young people sacrificed much more than the others in giving up food. They also were most adamant that the fast continue as long as it was necessary. One cannot help being impressed by the commitment of such young people. At such an early age they have understood the great commandment of love without having gone through catechesis. They have made options to serve the people without the benefit of the education for justice offered in Catholic schools. Most are so poor they've reached only the elementary grades in public schools.

They didn't learn about love and commitment and selflessness from the church, from the state, from the schools or other institutions. It was the result of their awakening to the contradictions around them. They have rejected the superficiality and hypocrisy of their elders who control and dominate the institutions of society and who cannot teach them about love beyond mere words. They will rally around the youthful leadership of a movement where they find their ideals being nourished, their expectations being considered, and their hopes finding promise of fulfillment.

They are young men and women who, like the prophets and martyrs, are willing to offer their lives so that others may live more fully. For some, Jesus of Nazareth is their inspiration. Even for those for whom he is not, the gospel is still fulfilled and the spirit of God's justice lives!

For the disciple, the ultimate hope lies in the unfolding of God's kingdom. Beyond the sorrow, sickness, and hunger, beyond the depressions, defeats, and disasters of this present world is the fulfillment of the words of the prophets that in the days to come Yahweh will reign. The universe and everything and everyone in this world will be transformed accordingly. We are not of course referring to that kind of heaven which has served as an escape from the concerns of our present life and society. Rather we look forward to God's reign in our own world within our own universe. As we struggle to become liberated from the greed, absolute power, and dominance of the few who control millions of people and as we struggle to be liberated from dehumanization and marginalization, we come to realize that the reign of God is close at hand.

5

Diary of a Fast

**So we fasted and besought our God. . . .
And God listened to our entreaty [Ezra 8:23].**

*The close to sixty detainees at the detention center in Davao City
began a fast on June 12, 1983, "to protest the violation of our rights
as political detainees." The fast lasted for thirty-three days until
July 14 when, since their demands had not been met, the group
decided to declare a full hunger strike. For the benefit of friends,
Karl kept a diary of the first week of the fast.*

JUNE 12

It was at Mass today that we formally announced our fast to
relatives and friends and the military who were present. We were
pleased with the liturgical celebration especially as those present
were touched. Despite the difficulty of communication between
cells, we managed to assign different tasks to each other and all
flowed smoothly as a result. Not only the talents of our companions impressed us, but also their courage to speak out militantly.
Oca, for example, read a rather militant poem. The climax of it all
was when, following the announcement of the fast, Sergeant Ál-
varez commanded us back to our cells. He shouted as he banged the
doors on us and everyone was taken aback. This act became a
symbol of the brutal responses of the military. The solemnity of the
liturgy was in sharp contrast to this harsh act, and it only served to
deepen the detainees' commitment to fast.

Diary of a Fast

By the time we returned to our cells we were very much relieved. The relief was primarily due to the military suspecting nothing. We had worried that there might be a leak of our plans and that the military would not allow us to have the Mass. It would not have been easy to launch the fast with such an impact if we had had to vary our plans in any way.

Clearly the soldiers had been caught offguard. During that part of the liturgy when we announced the fast, they were all over the place, buzzing around, unable to decide what to do. They then called the CO. He came and tried to restore order. We heard later, when we were once more padlocked, that a group of soldiers had been assembled outside because the detainees were "holding a demonstration." We also heard that Lieutenant Humol told Father Michel, who comes here regularly to celebrate Mass, that he will not be allowed to return if the liturgy is "used as a demonstration." We still don't know how Father Michel responded to this. We hope he is not easily threatened. To refuse to allow a priest to celebrate Mass here would be another violation of our rights. If they persist they will just add one more reason for our indefinite fast.

By the afternoon we were already receiving feedback from the other cells as to who had actually started to fast. We were very encouraged by the response. Out of a total of fifty-three detainees, thirty-nine are solidly supportive and, as the seven Muslims are fasting anyway because of *Ramadhan,* only seven are not with us. Most of those seven are either military detainees or are sick. All nine women are with us. We hope to encourage the Muslims but, realistically, only a few probably will persist with us. This is the problem here; we really are a mixed group. We are not one solid group of politicized detainees arrested because of our involvement in justice work. The military are also detained and could be used as spies to report on our activities inside the cells.

We heard from the other cells that morale is high, although the young boys find it rough. It is difficult for seventeen- and eighteen-year-olds to fast. They're the most vulnerable, though we are lucky to have some very strong boys here. The girls have decided to have common activities during the day. This challenged the others to discuss their own collective activities. There were discussions held throughout the night on how to encourage one another and how to get the relatives to be more involved.

Early this morning the guards wanted to take Oca out of our cell. When the guard came to transfer him to another cell, Oca refused and we supported him. We were afraid of a *hulbot*. To avoid a *hulbot*, we all acted as escorts as Oca was transferred to Cell 1. The kids were happy to see all of us at Cell 1. Once assured that Oca was safe, we returned to our own cell.

Today we are prepared to discuss the negotiations. We hope they won't *hulbot* some of us out of the detention center, and we pray that God will give us strength and courage to continue. Please keep vigil with us.

JUNE 13

This is our second day of fasting and the harassment continues. We were informed through reliable sources that I will not be allowed sunning with the rest of my companions in the cell. We, as a group, immediately decided that we will all refuse to go out. However, they still allowed me to visit with my mother. She came around 9:00 A.M. As soon as I was out in the visiting area I was informed that I could not receive her in the usual place as they did not want me to interact with other parents and detainees. So we were isolated from the rest. After thirty minutes, she was asked to leave.

Then there was another rumor. I was to be pulled out and transferred to another jail. For the whole day and night I waited for the transfer, but it never came. At first, I was very affected by the rumor, quite worried as to where they would transfer me, and not welcoming the possibility of being incommunicado again. I've become used to community life here, and it would be hard to be detained alone. But the anxiety quickly disappeared as I reflected on the need to be strong during this fast. I will have to offer more sacrifices. I have been here for two and a half months and I figure the worst has happened. The most they can really do is isolate me. They'll be afraid to touch me or to keep me away from my family and lawyers. They've learned their lesson. In a way, perhaps, I do have some "protection." Thanks to all the noise created over my disappearance.

Deceitful propaganda has been spread amongst us by the guards who used their stooges for this. The other cells were informed that we had taken food during lunch, and we were told that all the detainees in one cell had ended their fast. We were able to correct this right away so the propaganda wasn't effective.

Earlier, during my mother's visit, Colonel Superable sent a memo. It said that we would not be allowed to have Mass anymore because Sunday's liturgy was a "teach-in to attack government agencies and to win over to the left the other prisoners, even those just accused of petty crimes." Finally, the threat has become official. They have decided to take God away from us because they couldn't accept the God we worshiped on June 12. They want us to worship their god, whose eyes are closed to the concrete problems of the people. The memo increased our vigilance. Still another memo came. Sunning will be cut down to thirty minutes and can only be in small groups so that those accused of subversion will be separated from those charged with petty crimes.

The lack of media coverage affected the morale of the prisoners. We were expecting the radio and the local papers to cover the fast and were wondering what led to this news blackout. In the afternoon we learned that local media coverage had not been pursued by the support group because they feared that some of us might be hit. We let it be known that they should not worry about us because the local media coverage is very important for morale and that much more work needs to be done to publicize the fast. We hope this coverage will now improve in the coming days.

JUNE 14

Finally, the radio has reported the event here. It was the first local media coverage of our fast and we were grateful. More people will now know about our fast and the top military officials might start considering negotiating with us. But the events of the day showed that they hardened instead. There was another memo from Col. Superable reiterating that sunning will be on a staggered basis and that those accused of subversion/rebellion will not be mixed with those accused of petty crimes. We in our cell will have another schedule. Superable referred to us in his memo as "the hard core."

However, when I went out to meet my mother, I saw that the memo about staggered sunning was ignored. I guess even Col. Superable does not have full control over his men. Before my mother came, we heard a rumor that "the hard core" (a term we had fun using over and over again) will be transferred to Ma-a jail. This rumor persisted until nightfall.

My mother and I were again isolated from the rest. The guards remained very strict with the thirty-minute visit limit. After twenty minutes, the guard told me to go back to my cell because the visit was over. I said I still had ten minutes. He got mad and shouted at me: "Why are you so hardheaded?" I replied: "I still have a right to ten minutes and I intend to enjoy this right." He checked with the guard as to the time my mother arrived, and it was pointed out that I still had ten minutes. So the guard kept quiet, and I continued with my visit for another ten minutes.

Word came that we were going to have official visitors. One of the guards warned us that they might confiscate our ball pens, papers, pencils, and envelopes. I thought: "They've taken our music and our God, and now they'll take away our notes and letters." As it turned out, the visitors didn't come. When our turn for sunning came, I was again told that I couldn't go out. Most of my cell mates, however, didn't stay too long in the sun. I miss my jogging and I can feel the lack of exercise in my bones, but one has to accept the repercussions of an action. I compensated by doing more yoga exercises.

The guys are holding on extremely well. We have not heard of anyone giving up the fast and morale is still high. The news article printed in the *Mindanao Daily Mirror* greatly helped. When my mother brought a copy, everyone out for sunning milled around to read the news items. Nothing like "being in the papers" to feel somehow important. My brother also came to see me, and the three of us spent the visit catching up on family matters.

Father Dong's parents came to see him late this morning. He and Amy enclosed our "fast badge" in the letters they gave them. These were confiscated. The military are after our symbol now. They are on the defensive and so they constantly react. But it does show the power of symbols. So far we've not been able to have a common activity with our relatives because we are so dispersed and our communications lines have been weakened. But the commitment of our companions is very impressive. Even the Muslims have not been able to get over the fact of our *Duyog Ramadhan,* and they now realize that Christians can also take fasting seriously and can fast not merely for religious purposes but also for political reasons. I hope to have a chance later to reflect on and discuss the significance of fasting with them. So far we have been cut off from them and have had no opportunity for discussion.

This afternoon Attorney Bello came to see Volker and me. We went over some legal questions with him and asked him to follow up our request with Attorney Europa. My sister also came and this time she was allowed to see me in the visiting area. . . . Before taking our supper a frenzy of physical exercises took place in our cell. After supper we discussed what Lieutenant Colonel Lacanilao had told Attorney Bello—that "only the Muslims are fasting because of *Ramadhan*." Do the military leaders really think the people don't read the papers or listen to the radio? Do they really think they can always get away with their lies?

JUNE 15

Our fourth day. There exists an even stronger determination among the detainees to maintain the fast in spite of the refusal of the military to negotiate. There are some minor problems as a few prisoners, especially those accused of petty crimes, are being intimidated by the military, but by and large the men and women who are fasting remain firm and strong.

We in our cell, the so-called "hard-core," were to be the first out for sunning. However, the guard said that the order remained the same and I was not to be allowed out. My companions again refused to leave the cell and we decided to write Lieutenant Humol a letter informing him of our action. The others in Cell 1 also refused to enjoy their sunning to be in solidarity with me. To our surprise, less than thirty minutes after the letter was delivered Humol came to our cell and informed me that there was no such order from above and that I, too, could be out in the grounds.

Then he added that the military cannot grant our demands for two hours sunning in the morning and another two hours in the afternoon, along with visits of friends and other relatives. I told him that was our demand and one reason for our fasting, and until our demands are met we will keep on with our fast. Then he said, "Please do not write to your friends outside about conditions here." He left in a hurry, quite peeved by the exchange of words.

The guard stayed behind and was apologetic. We told him it was not his fault; there is clearly a problem of communication among the officers.

This interchange amused us and we enjoyed our small victory. The guard opened the cell immediately and allowed us out. Word reached the other cells and it raised morale. The military is still not quite sure how to react but it is definitely on the defensive.

We did our first jogging in four days.

When my mother came to visit me, we were again isolated from the rest. Once back in the cell after sunning and meeting with our visitors, we exchanged the information we had gained. There was a report that one of the guards had attempted to sow dissension in Cell 1. He had told them that the leaders were enjoying their supper and eating sardines and were not depending on the agreed ration. Of course the guys in Cell 1 realized he was only creating trouble. Still, we decided that we will refuse what our visitors bring except some biscuits and fruits. The news item which appeared in the *Mindanao Daily Mirror* was very much welcomed.

It was reported that in one cell all accept the rations even if three out of the seven have joined the fast. Apparently the three have been intimidated by the other four, especially by the military detainee. It is feared that this guy reports everything to the officers in order to delay his transfer to Muntinlupa, the national penitentiary in Luzon. He has been sentenced to twelve to sixteen years for murder.

The fear of *hulbot* remains very real, so guys in Cell 1 have decided that if a detainee is pulled out by the R2 they will embrace the detainee and create a noise barrage. Not to be caught off guard they take turns staying awake. This is the level of concern!

This sense of mutual concern and encouragement is very strong. Each one shows concern for the others by sending notes of encouragement, checking on those who are sick, and asking each other's reactions to the fast. We do a daily assessment; today's assessment was full of hope and conviction.

Late this afternoon we had a number of distinguished visitors: Attorneys Ilagan, Bello, and Arellano, who wanted to know the status of our fast. Fiscal Duerte came to ask the reason for the fast. Attorney Ilagan mentioned that one of the top military officers had asked him to persuade us not to create too much disturbance as we have no reason to complain about our prison conditions. Apparently we are causing the military headaches. Oh well, someone's bound to get them!

JUNE 16

At 8:00 A.M. the "hard core" was informed that they were to be first for the sunning schedule. Most were still asleep. Everyone joked that we should write Lieutenant Humol that we don't want our sunning at 8:00 since a number are still sleeping at that time. We wondered how Humol would react to this!

As agreed the previous day, we were going to sing out in the open in order to have some kind of communication with the others and to encourage one another to hold on. After jogging we sat down in the shade near Cells 1 and 3. We started singing *"Silayan,"* and progressed on to *"Ibong Malaya"* and *"Pag-ibig Sa Tinubuang Lupa."* As expected, those in Cells 1 and 3 understood the message and responded accordingly.

Later on, the detainees from Cell 1 also put on a spontaneous concert while out in the sun. They sang mostly *Asin* songs and they sang very loudly so everyone could hear them. Across from us is the tall Maguindanao Hotel. An appreciative fan from the hotel window clapped his hands. The delighted detainees and even the guards joined in the fun. This was a breakthrough as it encouraged us to find our solidarity in songs—something which does not threaten our captors.

Communication by word of mouth is still difficult. The military detainees post themselves in the visiting area making interaction difficult. They watch our every move, and are the source of inside information for their superiors. There should be a law which prevents the mixing of genuine political prisoners with petty criminals including undisciplined soldiers. The latter just don't have any sense of conscience—all they want is favor and privilege, a pat on the back from their superiors and release from prison by taking advantage of their position to harm the genuine prisoners of conscience. They're worse than parasites!

We checked out the health and morale of our fellow fasters. Except for three girls with gum problems, we did not hear of any health problems. Morale remains high. The men in one cell are being pressured to accept food. We encouraged them not to be afraid of the police in their cell and to refuse the food. Those who were accepting food from relatives were discouraged from doing so. Communication from outside was shared with everyone for mutual encouragement.

Nothing major had come from the outside. No local or national news coverage, no important visitors, and no update on international support. There was also no major harassment from inside. All the military did was become more strict with visitors by not allowing them to bring their bags into the visiting area. There was some disappointment and depression among us. Despite this, we thought we were on the offensive as no major problems had come up to create tensions among ourselves. The military is biding its time. It is using soft tactics without yielding an inch. Our hope lies in the pressure from outside, especially from national and international circles. We can't do anything else apart from holding on.

There is hope that our relatives can meet again to discuss building up their own pressure and that the IBP will move. We prayed that the TFDP would follow up our national and international friends. We sent out messages ourselves to mobilize all possible external support. We fervently hope that our friends won't give up their vigil with us.

Letters of support arrived and they were very much appreciated.

JUNE 17

This is the sixth day of our fast. The day was uneventful except for a few minor happenings. I was late for my court hearing (my guards forgot about my schedule), but I managed to catch up and I saw friends who were still around. There was also news! Amnesty International U.S. and Canada have been informed about our fast. TFDP Manila has also relayed this information to other foreign friends. Negotiations are still in the pipeline to have Mass celebrated on Sunday. The local media friends have refuted Superable's claims concerning our "use" of it, and the relatives and the lawyers were to do the necessary follow-up with the authorities.

When I got back from the court, I shared all this with the others who were very much encouraged. A minor problem came up when a note sent by the girls was confiscated. It was a rather harmless note but the military is good at making mountains out of anthills. We also sent the poem read during last Sunday's liturgy to the girls and that, too, was confiscated.

By noontime, the guards wanted to pull Mario out of his cell. His companions all stood firm around him and resisted the guards' attempt. The guards, acting on orders from the R2, threatened Mario but the detainees didn't move an inch, so nothing happened. On hearing this I reflected that we may not get the military to respond to our demands, but we have developed a sense of unity and mutual protection. We have broken away from the paralysis of fear, and we will not allow the military to throw its weight around. No one will be pulled out from now on. If the soldiers attempt to force a detainee to go with them there will be forceful resistance along with a noise barrage. This action is very symbolic because it shows all of us the need to go on struggling and it has provided some assurance that the *hulbot*s will stop. In spite of the hunger, there are more detainees who can now sleep well.

There was again a lot of singing during our sunning. The intrigues have also stopped since we confronted those who were allowing themselves to be used by their own captors. No rumors either. Most have gotten used to the fast but we're still worried some might become sick. But all in all the morale remains high and the commitment strong.

JUNE 18

Another day of waiting. We wondered how long we will have to fast before our captors make a move to respond to our demands. There is still no sign that they are willing to negotiate.

During our sunning in the early morning, we noticed that they were erecting a barbed wire fence in the visiting area. They want us far away from our relatives when they come to visit us. It is the hope of the military that the two barbed wire fences—an arm's length from each other—will limit communication between the detainees and relatives. It will be difficult to talk in whispers or to pass on information, and the visiting area will be a circus once the fence is up. To further cut down on communication between us and relatives, the guards and their *alalays* position themselves within hearing distance. They are so rude in their methods and they take little trouble to be subtle. Big brother cannot afford to place a secret microphone in the visiting area so he personally positions himself there!

We're not surprised. As we push them to the negotiating table, the military will try to push us to the corner, and they will inflict stricter rules and procedures in the detention center. All they have is brute, physical power that stems from their fascistic and repressive authority. We have moral power. That is our advantage.

As expected, there are problems with the guys who do not have the discipline or stamina to face the consequences of collective decisions, but we try to continue to provide all the support possible. One guy in Cell 1 is suffering from an ulcer. His cell mates are helping him out. We wonder whether we can have the doctor soon. The rest of the day we discussed what to do on Sunday, with or without the Mass. By late afternoon we heard there will be a Mass, but celebrated by the military chaplain. We decided to be silent, except at the end. Our silence will be an eloquent sign of protest at the military's use of the Mass to violate our religious rights!

JUNE 27: LETTER TO JIM WALLIS

. . . Today is the sixteenth day of our fast and we are still holding on. The morale is high among the group. There has been a lot of outside support—a number of friends here and abroad have joined us in the fast and friends and relatives have been mobilizing support. We may not reach forty days and forty nights of fasting, since negotiations with the military have begun, but then the procedures of the authorities usually take a long time, so it might still be a week or two before we end our fast.

JULY 9

After a month of fasting, the group decided to declare a full hunger strike since there had been no attempt on the part of the authorities to respond to the demands of the fasters.

AN OPEN LETTER

Davao MetroDisCom PC/INP Jail
Davao City

On Thursday, July 14, we, the Political Prisoners at the Davao MetroDisCom PC/INP Jail, Davao City, will declare a hunger strike! We have been waiting for the local military authorities, primarily Colonel Andres Superable, to respond to our demands for prison reforms, as well as our rights, as we fasted. On July 13, we will have fasted for thirty-two days.

There has been no word from Colonel Superable, nor any attempt on his part to dialogue with us. The most he has done is to provide some token offerings. He came to "dialogue" with two groups—first, with the women detainees, and, second, with one group of the men prisoners. In the second session, the prisoners kept quiet. We later informed Colonel Superable that we will talk with him if he meets everybody as one group, rather than in small groups. We also informed him in a letter dated July 5 that we will only end our fast if our minimum expectations are met, based on a genuine dialogue with him to be attended by a few relatives and legal counsel.

We have not received any response from Colonel Superable. It looks as if he couldn't care less about our demands despite the sacrifice we have undertaken. In order to express our seriousness in pursuing the struggle for our rights, we will go from a fast to a hunger strike!

Beginning July 14, we will refuse to accept food. We will give up the one meal we have been taking since June 12. We will boycott our one-hour sunning session to further dramatize our demands.

Ramadhan ends on July 11. Our Muslim detainees have signified their solidarity. They, too, will join in the hunger strike. Even those who have suffered pain as a result of the long fast are joining. Of course not everyone will join us, as there are military detainees and others accused of petty crimes who are not genuine political prisoners. But two-thirds of the total number of political prisoners have decided to declare this hunger strike as a last resort.

We call on our relatives, friends in media, the religious, the human rights groups, our legal counsel, those who have stood by us through the fast (WATCH, PNA, MSPC, Friends of the Detainees, TFDP, etc.) to intensify their vigil with us. If the military authorities still refuse to dialogue with us and to respond to our demands, we will continue with the hunger strike. Some of us may not have the capacity to be without food for days, so we will need medical attention, even hospitalization. We deeply appreciate the support you have shown since we started our fast, and we know that we will be needing your support even more when the emergency comes.

We hope that something can be done to avert any tragic consequences. But we have reached the point where we cannot just sit back and wait. Enough is enough!

> THE POLITICAL PRISONERS
> Davao MetroDisCom PC/INP Jail
> Davao City

JULY 17

You must have heard that five Sundays ago, on June 12, we began a fast in order to struggle for our rights as political prisoners. Apart from token offerings, the military authorities have been unwilling to grant our demands. After our thirty-three day fast, we decided to declare a full hunger strike, beginning on July 14. This is our fourth day, the hunger pangs are becoming more intense and a number are getting sick but not seriously enough to require a doctor. Our captors may do a Thatcher act—"Let Bobby Sands die, we won't give up." On the other hand, and this is our hope, they might capitulate when they have a dying person on their bloody hands. On the fourth day, morale is still strong.

On July 13, we sent a letter to Colonel Andres Superable. He is the MetroDisCom chief who administers the detention center, and we informed him that we were going to start our hunger strike the following day. Less than an hour after receiving the letter he came to dialogue with all of us together for the first time since we fasted. We went through the demands, but he was in such a hurry to end the session that we felt cheated. The following day we were allowed to meet as one body by ourselves to find out whether our minimum expectations had been met. They had not, so the decision to hold a strike held.

On Friday, July 15, they canceled the sunning schedule and pad-locked us the whole day. Visitors, however, were allowed to see the prisoners. Our relatives told us that they planned to see Colonel Superable that morning. Since communications have been cut off we don't know whether they were able to see him and, if so, what came out of their meeting. On Saturday, they padlocked us again the whole day, and no relatives were allowed to visit. There was red alert inside the military camp. In the morning, they arrested close to three hundred people who joined a march in the city denouncing the worsening economic situation and militarization. They were kept inside the camp the whole day before being released last night. Three, however, whom they suspect to be leaders, are still detained. One is an old man who was tortured.

. . . It is now raining, which reinforces the gloom in the cells, a gloom partly attributable to hunger pains and partly to having again been deprived of the opportunity of being together on a Sunday morning. Something deep in us says that Sundays are for picnics and for having fun! Peter, my Muslim cell mate, was out in the visiting area early this morning to take care of the garbage. He reported later that the old man arrested and tortured yesterday was allowed to see his daughter who was carrying her child. She was crying. The child was also crying. The father couldn't help but also cry. In that moment three generations shared the pain and anguish of a country in turmoil, a people in struggle.

Having gone through a lonely hunger strike all by myself in the Davao City safehouse and the small dark cell at Bago Bantay during the first two weeks of my detention, I'm glad that this time I am with others. Somehow suffering is more bearable when shared. It doesn't take away the hunger pains, but the will to move on is strengthened. . . .

Thank you for your continuing prayers and concern. To those who write letters, thank you. I'm sorry I'm not able to answer immediately, given our precarious situation. Your solidarity through these trying times is most appreciated. We hope nothing tragic will happen before our demands are met. We cross our fingers in the hope that we won't have to go through a forty-day and forty-night hunger strike. While that is biblically sound, I wonder if anyone of us here has the strength and stamina to stay alive that long.

As I was ending this letter, a guard came rushing to our cell to borrow our "polar bear," because one of the girls, Eva, had collapsed. I heard Jethro coughing nearby, and I pray that he gets a good night's sleep so he will be stronger in the morning. Across, Celio is holding on but is haunted by the memory of being rushed to a hospital because of acute ulcers. Nathaniel, my cell mate, along with Peter and Vol, is so weak that he is almost totally still. I wonder how his wife, Virgie, in Cell 3, is and what's on her mind having five very young girls with her in the cell.

It is night as I finish this letter. The rain has stopped. It is only 7:44 P.M. but the cells are unusually quiet. The radio softly echoes the song's lyrics "at the end of the storm, is a golden sky. . . . " We'll walk on through the rain, knowing that tomorrow the sun will shine.

I end with prayer that we may all survive the fascist storms!

JULY 21

Greetings of peace from another cell of another prison!

So many things have happened since my last letter of July 17, the most important happening yesterday. Just after 1:00 in the afternoon, Volker and I were transferred from the Davao MetroDis-Com PC/INP Detention Center to the Davao City Jail, around eight kilometers away. The Davao City Jail (DCJ) is for criminal prisoners. Why the transfer? Our guess is the local military are finding the international pressure and support for our hunger strike too much. Perhaps they think the leadership behind the hunger strike will collapse once we are out of there and that they can then facilitate the resolution of the strike.

The order which we were allowed to read came from the local military regional command informing those in the detention center to look into our transfer to any detention center in Metro Manila, and, while this is being explored, to place us temporarily at DCJ. We were unable to resist the order, of course, and the most we can do is inform our lawyers. When we arrived here the warden, Captain Emmanuel Mesias (oh God, what have they done to your name?), immediately received us and gave a very emphatic order: "While you are here, you are supposed to follow prison rules." We were then brought to our cell. We informed him that they needn't

bother sending us food since we are on hunger strike.

We are in Cell 2 and there are six other inmates who are all very young. The youngest is fifteen and the oldest is twenty-three. The youngest kid has been convicted of rape with homicide and is due to be transferred to Manila. He really looks like an eight-year-old kid. The others are accused of drug crimes, theft and robbery, carnapping, and various petty crimes. They're a bunch of nice kids, eager to please, and deprived of so many things. They're born-again Christians and are proud to be charismatics. We joined in their Bible sharing last night (with mixed emotions).

Our family and counsel have been allowed to see us. We have been informed of the actions being taken on our behalf. We are grateful. Somehow, outside support is the vitamin that keeps both body and spirit intact. Volker and I are only drinking water, and we explained to the six kids why we are on a hunger strike. They tried to understand. Later, they told the other prisoners about us. After eight days of hunger strike, following a thirty-three day fast, the body starts to feel the effects. I am getting to be quite lazy, almost always lying down. I can't really sleep as much as I want to, partly because of the noise here, although last night it wasn't too bad so I had enough sleep. Volker and I are sharing a very small bed so I woke up with a painful back from the cramps I had in the night. I am beginning to find reading and writing tiresome, so I do very little of both. Fortunately, we have access to a window which looks out upon a very green view of the Ma-a hills and plains. A beautiful sight indeed since in the other jail we saw only walls.

There are certain things here that are much better than in the other jail: there is no *hulbot*; the food, we're told, is better (the prisoners here go on a noise barrage if the food is awful); the jailers are more liberal with visitors, except with us, naturally; and religious services are regular. However, the rooms are much more congested; the sunning is not daily; the cottage industry projects have been suspended as the pastor of the UCCP, who was here to oversee the ecumenical project, had a clash with the warden; there are no conjugal rights. The prisoners should really declare a hunger strike here, too. How does one motivate criminal inmates to struggle for their rights? But I hope they won't do it while we are still here, or we will be blamed as the agitators!

AUGUST 1, 1983

A few days after Karl and Volker were transferred, the hunger strike came to an end.

Sunday, July 24, came. We were informed that the new Metro-DisCom commander, Colonel Valderama (who had taken over from Colonel Superable) had a dialogue with the political prisoners at the detention center concerning our demands. From what we were told, the colonel showed an openness toward meeting our minimum expectations. However, he needed time to work out the implementation of the reforms in prison. In order to express good-will and trust in his word, the detainees decided to lift the hunger strike as of the afternoon of July 24. We were informed the following day and so we started eating on Monday. The detainees, however, informed the colonel that they were still demanding our transfer back to the detention center. A week has passed but we're still here in the city jail.

It was a rather long fast. For thirty-three days beginning last June 12 we ate only our supper consisting of a glass of rice and a small fish. When the authorities refused to grant our demands, we declared a full hunger strike on July 14. We ate nothing for eleven days until our captors capitulated. From what we have heard, the reforms are now being implemented, especially the following: return of beds and furniture, regular Sunday liturgy, adequate sunning, better food, regular medical service, more liberal rules related to visitors, and facilitation of the release of those who should already be freed. Our other demands are to be followed up by the Integrated Bar of the Philippines (IBP), Davao chapter. We are still awaiting a signed statement by the military commander that will guarantee full implementation of the reforms.

There were mixed emotions and reactions to the end of the hunger strike. There was of course relief for both detainees and relatives. The long fast had taken its toll, in loss of weight and sickness. The day we were transferred here I got sick and my health deteriorated. The night before the hunger strike was over, I thought I would have to be rushed to the hospital; I was so sick I thought I

wouldn't survive. Even now, a week since we started eating, I still feel very weak. We heard there are others at the detention center who also got sick and who will need time to fully recover.

There also remains a sense of insecurity as to whether the military authorities will keep their word. Many experiences in the past have shown that promises of prison reform were not kept. Rules change as the personalities in charge of the detention center also change. Even if there are rules, some of the guards blatantly ignore these and trample on the rights of prisoners. If a minor event occurs within the camp, procedures are immediately suspended. At times even the moods of our captors determine the regulations. A sense of cynicism frequently grips those who have been detained for a longer time, even as they continue to struggle for their rights in prison.

There is a tremendous feeling, though, of appreciation for all who have kept vigil with us, especially our relatives who refused to succumb to harassment and threat. Unfortunately, there were those who did succumb to pressure and became unwitting instruments of our captors in their campaign to discourage their detainee-relative on hunger strike. We are most grateful to our friends, some of our legal counsel, and those institutions that backed us up at a time when we desperately needed outside support. Those who fasted along with us also gave us much needed encouragement. We were also informed of the international solidarity which intensified through the weeks of our fasting, and we were very touched. If we remained strong till the end, our strength flowed from the support, concern, prayers, and affection we received from relatives and friends. Their strength gave us the courage to continue despite the hunger, which used to become intolerable at nights when we couldn't sleep and despite the fear of reprisal and insecurity of not knowing whether the whole affair would be resolved without tragic consequences.

Throughout the fast and hunger strike the military authorities adopted all kinds of tactics in order to negate the moral impact of the fast. They lied to media, harassed relatives, threatened those detainees who were most vulnerable, and made promises to those most gullible. It was not surprising, therefore, that a number of detainees, who were with us at the start of the fast, had dropped out by the time of the hunger strike. But up to the very end

of the hunger strike, our captors were confronted with a group of thirty-five detainees who refused to surrender. In the end they had no choice but to yield to our demands. It took a lot out of us, but in the end our struggle was worth it! We scored a moral victory!

Since this is not a fairy tale, the prospect of prison reforms will not make us live happily ever after. Still, if there is a sincere effort on the part of the military authorities to implement the reforms, our life behind bars will be more tolerable. The detainees will need to remain vigilant in fighting for their rights, for nothing is given out of generosity and humanness by our captors. The stark lesson of our fast and hunger strike is that in a repressive society the people have to struggle for their rights. Basic human rights in our context will never be offered to us on a silver platter by those in power.

The forty-four day fast and hunger strike provided moments of prayer and reflection. . . . What happened to us as a community through those hungry days is but a reflection of what is happening in the broader Philippine society. There are more and more people who are willing to take the risk and undergo sacrifices for their rights and for the good of all. . . . If only because it provided us with time and space to show that we are concerned for each other's welfare, that we care for each other's well-being, and that we hope for each other's safety, it was well worth the hunger, risks, and anxiety.

Other insights also surfaced as to the prophetic value of a fast. I understand the meaning of the gospel account of Jesus' fast for forty days in the desert a little better. The words of the prophet Second Isaiah linking fasting and justice (chap. 58) have gained a clarity and intensity that call for commitment to the biblical call to justice. I also appreciate the Muslims' *Ramadhan* and hope that fasting can be taken more seriously by Christians in the context of the prophetic words of Second Isaiah. Hunger in the gut makes one fully experience the dehumanizing consequences of hunger that the poor face daily. The struggle against poverty and injustice takes on a concrete physical praxis.

"The hand of our God is for good upon all that seek him, and the power of His wrath is against all that forsake Him." So we fasted and besought our God for this, and he listened to our entreaty [Ezra 8:22–23].

. . . I end with a paragraph written by a very young church worker who is searching for a meaningful role in our struggle which demands much from his generation:

But here is hope, as the old truism goes. Since I was fifteen, I've been awed and amazed by the sight of a sunset. I'd stand without saying anything, watching the colors burst into the sky. At the beach last year, the wet dunes were practically bathed in orange. From that time on, I knew that beauty was eternal and that God's most beautiful creation would not and could not be curtailed by any kind of institutionalized power, whether in the form of unjust laws, secret decrees, or even detention. I also know that if freedom should be considered as the core of beauty itself, then in all respects it knows no death.

I pray that we can all have the gift of good health, peace of mind and the courage of the prophets!

6

Liturgical Feasts and Celebrations

A church that refuses to be incarnated in the lives of the poor
and powerless has no right to claim to be witnessing to the
gospel. A church that celebrates the people's struggle to be
fully human by being in the center of this historical, creative
process is truly Christ's legacy for his followers through the
ages.

K. Gaspar

THE BEHEADING OF JOHN THE BAPTIST—AUGUST 29

Today is the commemoration of the beheading of John the
Baptist. Unfortunately, it is not as popular a feast as June 24, his
birthday, when, in a travesty of folklore, people remember him by
going to the beach or throwing water at people in buses. A prophet
who denounced lies and injustices and was murdered by the
powers-that-be reduced into a reason for swimming and throwing
water! How tragic!

The fact is that John the Baptist could be the most relevant saint
for Third World churches, next to the Blessed Mother and Joseph
the Worker. This is especially true for the persecuted churches in
repressive Third World countries where so many Christians are
being called upon to follow the example of both John and his
cousin, our Lord. The contemporary John the Baptists are everywhere: Oscar Romero and the four American churchwomen in El
Salvador, the Indian catechists of Guatemala, the students in

Kwangju, the workers in Chile, the blacks in South Africa, Agatep and other church workers in the Philippines. Each time a person dares point his or her finger at the people's oppressors to denounce their lies and corruption and to unmask the hypocrisy of the established order there is a John the Baptist. Whenever people risk their lives for the sake of truth, the spirit of John lives again.

John Paul II said: "The lie is at the root of violence, and a search for truth is the work of peacemakers!" As a voice from the wilderness, John came to prepare the way for the Lord's coming as he announced the coming of the kingdom. He preached repentance and penance. He did not hesitate to name names and say who should be on their knees to ask God's forgiveness for their sins against God and the people. Naturally, he got into trouble when his finger pointed to the palace of the elite. He was no reed who would be blown by the wind in any direction (Matt. 11:7), rather he stood firm on his prophetic ground and never vacillated. The inevitable culmination of a prophet's life came: he was arrested. When his enemies saw they would only be secure with his "silence," they plotted for his head. They got it on a silver platter for the price of a dance.

John would feel at home in our kind of society! The lies being perpetuated have become so obvious to ordinary people. We have become a society fed on untruths and half-truths. The main institutions of society—government, military, schools, and mass media—are in collusion to hide the truth from the people. Every day there are more lies—witness how the media has concealed the truth or fabricated lies about the Manotoc kidnapping, President Marcos's health, Mrs. Marcos's wealth, the number of political prisoners and salvaged victims, the wedding at Sarrat, favors to cronies, the U.S. military bases agreement, the Westinghouse nuclear power plant deal, the IMF-WB connection, the Haig deal for helicopters, the three weeks' leave of the president to write a book, and the assassination of Aquino to mention only a few! Lies have become a way of life. How can a people believe in a government that has become so crude in lying? Its hold on power is through lies. Naturally, violence, the product of insecurity and lies, is very much present in the conduct of state affairs. Human rights and civil liberties are inevitably violated for the sake of the lie. Anyone who speaks the truth becomes a national security threat and is labeled an enemy of the state. A "peacemaker" will very probably end up like John the Baptist.

God has gifted us with prophets throughout all our history and we are grateful for the legacy of heroism. Today we have José Diokno, the women journalists, the Mabini lawyers, the religious women, student and labor leaders, small Christian community leaders, Bishop Labayen and many other human rights advocates— the list is impressive. Oh, a thousand more!

How many of us are really ready to risk ourselves for the sake of truth and justice? Maybe the reason for reducing John the Baptist's feastday to picnics and throwing water is because it is difficult to cope with the example he gave us which led to his beheading. He is just too militant and too radical for us! But what happened to John was just a prelude to the Suffering Servant's death on the cross. And he asked us to follow him. Can we muster the courage to embrace our own cross? Some of our countrymen and country-women have said yes and they're leading the way for us. We can only pray that we will be blessed with the grace of faith to survive the test when our turn comes. And when it comes, may we have the courage and the fire of the prophets!

FEAST OF THE ASSUMPTION—AUGUST 15

Today is your [Assumption Sisters of Davao] feastday celebration. As I have no gift, I thought that perhaps I can offer you some reflections as an expression of my being one with you all today.

Mary is truly with us and we see her face reflected in the faces of so many of our women who are undergoing the same pain and suffering that she herself endured. Mary knew poverty and deprivation. In accepting her role as mother of God she must have known uncertainty and deep insecurity. In Bethlehem she and Joseph had no money to pay for a room so they could find no decent place in which to stay. Their powerlessness is so like the situation of the women and children in Tondo who resisted the demolition team and whose anguished faces have been on the front pages of the *Bulletin Today* for these past few days.

As refugees, Mary and Joseph fled to Egypt to escape the soldiers who did not hesitate to massacre innocent children in their search for Jesus. How like our own refugees forced to leave the militarized zones and settle in strategic hamlets. They, too, are deprived of their rights as they flee from soldiers whose path spells death. The mothers in those hamlets, like Mary, suffer from inadequate shelter, lack of food, and sanitation problems, and they fear for the safety of their children.

But what was this anguish and anxiety compared to what followed? Following her son as he carried out his mission she was well aware of the risks. Her son's social nonconformity, his teachings, his life style and his prophetic options threatened those in power— even as he attracted more and more to follow him. True enough, at the prime of his life, Jesus was arrested, tortured, and executed. She was with him as he walked through the streets carrying his cross and was with him until his death as a victim of brutal violence inflicted by the powerful establishment. She was there, helpless, without any friends at the top who could intercede for her, without money to bargain for her son's life, with nothing but her love for and fidelity to a beloved son.

How many mothers from Argentina to South Korea, from Turkey to South Africa, from Chile to the Philippines, are sharing her harrowing ordeal? How many more will there be as repression and fascism continue unabated and as the machinery continues to justify such brutalities in the name of national security? How deep must be Mary's compassion for the mothers of the *desaparecidos* of Argentina, for the massacred students of Kwangju, for the salvaged suspected "subversives" of Mindanao, for the missing labor organizers of Santiago, and for all those whose lives ended with so much blood shed for justice and freedom. Today Mary stands with all the women in the world who are poor, deprived, and oppressed, offering her own solidarity. With them she is praying that God will intervene in the liberation of God's people from their poverty, human misery, and slavery under such powerful, abusive rulers. She certainly was no typical, apolitical matron whose only concern was piety and morality.

In the Magnificat, Luke has Mary speaking "revolutionary" language which is, according to Paul Winters, reminiscent of a Maccabean battle song:

He has shown might with his arm; he has confused the proud in their inmost thoughts. He has deposed the mighty from their thrones and raised the lowly to high places. To the hungry he has given every good thing, while the rich he has sent empty away [Luke 1:51–53].

Everything about Mary makes her the ideal spokesperson of the *anawim*. She is a woman with all the compassionate sensitivities often lacking in men, especially those in power. She has a heart that embraces the marginalized, lowly, and weak. As a mother, she instinctively feels for human life; she knows there will be drought and rain, good times and bad. She continues to dream and they are dreams of equality, justice, and solidarity.

Mary is truly our mother and definitely our closest ally. She is one with us in our suffering and in our struggle. In her assumption there is hope for all of us. Like her we will one day be gifted by God with our own resurrection. Despite the sufferings and misery of our people today, there will be the dawning of the new heaven and the new earth. The poor who are faithful to the gospel will enter the kingdom and experience, with Mary, all the joy and glory of a just and humane society.

This promise encourages us to face the present risks. It gives us hope to defeat our fears and sense of hopelessness. Our discipleship and servanthood bring us to a humble acceptance of the same pain and anguish which Mary accepted so freely and willingly as part of her own mission. Knowing Mary's love for her children, we believe that one day we shall overcome and we will see the kingdom: "Fear not, stand firm, and see the salvation of the Lord which he will work for you today" (Exod. 14:13).

I will end here as it is very late, and you are probably tired after reading this long letter.

Happy feastday! And may Mary teach you to sing more battle songs!

THE SACRAMENT OF SOLIDARITY

The highlight of our week is the Sunday liturgical celebration. All the prisoners, Christian and Muslim, civilian and military, believer and nonbeliever, look forward to it as it casts an air of peace over all the cells. When there is no liturgy, the day is gloomy and everyone feels lousy.

Many factors account for its popularity. On Sunday the only time we are allowed out of our cells is the hour for Mass. It is the one hour in the week when we can all get out together to see and greet each other, to come to know the newly padlocked detainees, and to meet our relatives and friends who are allowed to join us for the celebration.

The Sunday liturgy then symbolizes our unity. It is literally the occasion for oneness, for our gathering together as a community. It is the sacrament of our solidarity with one another and with our relatives and friends. When civilian priests are allowed to say Mass, we share in its preparation and the celebration is rich and meaningful. We bring to it our aspirations and anxieties, our hopes and struggles, our pain and friendship as offerings. God's presence within the boundaries of the prison becomes visible and real. Mass celebrated within barbed wire fences takes on a poignancy of its own as the memory of Christ nailed to the cross is made more intense. The barbed wire fences are symbols of the enforced divisions within our community as the men detainees are separated from the women and the prisoners are separated from their relatives and friends. These divisions are reflections of a society and a world divided along class, race, and sex lines that have become the basis for oppression and dehumanization. Christ's death and resurrection celebrated in the midst of these divisions is a foreshadowing of the kingdom where genuine unity will be achieved. The celebration becomes the outward sign of solidarity and of handholding together in the struggle for justice. Our situation denies us active participation in that struggle, but in our liturgy we remain linked. At the prayer of the faithful, peasants, workers, and all other marginalized and politicized groups are remembered that they might be strengthened to continue and to intensify their involvement in the social transformation of our country.

Unfortunately, as I write these reflections, only the military chaplain is allowed to come and say Mass. We will attend it, but the sacrament has been desecrated by the powers-that-be.

. . . Today, July 17, 1983, they are not going to allow us out of our cells to see our relatives. This clearly is a reprisal for our militant stand over the hunger strike. They have also refused us Mass for the second consecutive Sunday as no military chaplain is available. This refusal made headlines in the local daily newspaper the following day. Last Sunday they allowed a priest to distribute communion and he told us the reading for that day was the parable of the Good Samaritan. It seemed ironic that the military officer refused to allow Mass to be celebrated because he was fulfilling his own religious duties and could not be around to supervise. I wondered how he related to that gospel reading!

Colonel Superable was quoted as saying that he wouldn't allow civilian priests to say Mass here because they attack the government. A month ago he told the media that some of the detainees were using the Mass for Marxist teach-ins. We keep asking him to come and join us for the Mass and see for himself, but until now he has not come.

During our dialogue with the colonel on July 13, Pastor Volker took exception to his claim that our Masses were Marxist teach-ins. Naturally, the colonel had the last word, and he said that Mass should only be celebrated for spiritual upliftment. He must think we are a bunch of unbelievers as he insists on calling us communists.

But who are the unbelievers of our day? Are they not the "faithful" who attend Sunday services with blood on their hands from the torture and summary execution of those suspected of subversion? Are they not the people who publicize acts of kindness to the poor but are responsible for causing untold anguish to hundreds of peasants they force to move into strategic hamlets?

> When you spread forth your hands,
> I will hide my eyes from you;
> even though you make many prayers,
> I will not listen;
> your hands are full of blood.
> Wash yourselves; make yourselves clean;
> . . . cease to do evil, learn to do good;
> seek justice, correct oppression [Isa. 1:15–17a].

Can we call "unbelievers" those who may not claim to be faithful to their religious duties but are willing to offer their lives for the sake of their suffering fellow human beings? They may not take certain religious expressions seriously, but it is their passion for justice and freedom which is causing the powerful on their thrones to tremble.

A REFLECTION ON THE BEATITUDES

The reading in today's liturgy was the Beatitudes (Matt. 5:3-12). This celebrated passage stayed with me throughout Mass and is still with me. As this gospel passage was being read, I glanced at the people surrounding the altar. How many of them concretely manifested the promise of the Beatitudes?

There is this married woman, a civil servant. Nearly every Sunday she joins us for Mass with her husband and daughter. She adopted one of the detainees whose family was very poor and lived so far away that they could never visit or follow up the boy's case. The boy's family had already been a victim of militarization in their own barrio. Despite personal risks she followed up his case and eventually gained his release. Now she comes to see if she can help others. "Fortunate are those who are merciful to others; God will be merciful to them!"

Then there is a mother, quiet but eloquent in her quietness. Her face shows a life of suffering, and now she is here with her youngest who is a political prisoner. She did everything to gain money for his bail, cutting family expenses and borrowing money only to discover that her son is under a PDA and cannot be granted bail. She collapsed in the judge advocate's office on hearing this. "Fortunate are those who mourn; God will comfort them!"

Also beside the altar is one of our most recent arrivals, a fourteen-year-old kid, Manuelito, who was rounded up during a military operation. He has been charged with subversion and is considered a threat to national security! He is in a cell across from mine, and I have yet to see him get depressed or cry. One time I asked him how he found prison and he said, "It is not so bad; there's a lot of fun here!" Even as I write this letter, he is still awake strumming a guitar singing his favorite "message songs" despite an irritation in his right eye. Manuelito and the other youngsters are echoes of Nicaragua's *Los Niños*. "Fortunate are the pure of heart; they will see God!"

. . . Then there are the four priests who concelebrated our liturgy (Fathers Rey, Louie, Dong, and Dong Tizon). I felt proud that the church in the Philippines has produced such exemplary pastors. Each one has sought to commit himself where he could best serve the people. Collectively, they have concretized in their lives the desire to do God's will in our historical context which can only be in the upholding of justice and peace. "Fortunate are those who hear the Word of God and fulfill it" (Luke 11:28).

Meanwhile, thanks for keeping me in your thoughts, for your letters and gifts and for continuing to keep vigil with me. I pray that you will continue to be on the side of peace, will always proclaim the demands of justice and will ever be passionately in love with those who demand our kinship and solidarity.

> Fortunate are those who work for peace;
> God will call them his children.

ADVENT BEHIND BARS:
AWAITING THE DAWNING OF FREEDOM

There is no place more appropriate for the celebration of Advent than prison. The waiting is very intense. Liberation from captivity is passionately desired by the detainees. The anticipation of that day when they can freely walk out brings both pain and pleasure.

In this waiting, Advent becomes real. The Child is not yet born. Since the dawning of salvation history, God's chosen people waited for the One who would perfect God's reconciliation with all peoples. When God's hour came, the momentous event took place quietly, without fanfare. The birth was stark in its simplicity. It could have been the birth of a poor peasant's child in some Third World country.

We wait for Christmas and we wait for our release papers. These are not two separate events as they converge in our waiting for the Lord, who came to bring us justice and truth, the truth that will give freedom to all the Lord's children.

However, a detainee's long wait is but a minor footnote to the bigger concern of the people's liberation from the prison which society has become for them. Their waiting is filled with passion and hope. It may take years. It may not come with this generation or the next, but it will come. It will happen as surely as the birthday of the son of God. That birth came on a cold Christmas morning, and the people's liberation will come one bright dawn, signaling the new heaven and the new earth.

. . . In two weeks' time it will be Christmas. Already the mornings are nippy, and on most afternoons a pleasant breeze gently caresses the leaves of the *talisay* and *ipil-ipil* trees that surround the prison. With the December weather our cells are more bearable. We have put up the Christmas lanterns and decorations, and they have brought some color to the desolate landscape of the prison. In the last two weeks I have received hundreds of Christmas cards, mainly from England (thanks to Amnesty International), and they're pasted on a wall in our cell. It is quite a collage of Christmas images: Raphael's Madonna and Child, Picasso's flowers, doves of peace, Indian, Peruvian, Chinese, Japanese, Salvadoran interpretations of the Christmas event, white Christmas scenes, stars, the Three Kings, angels, and poinsettias. The cards convey only one message—have hope, you are not forgotten!

For all the heartaches experienced as Christmas is spent in prison, there is the consoling thought that the prison cell brings us closer to that Bethlehem scene. There is also the rare opportunity of being genuinely imbued with the spirit of poverty and of actually experiencing the physical ordeal of being deprived and impoverished. The lonely cell during some sleepless nights in the Christmas season becomes the stable to welcome again the coming of the prophet who declared liberty to the captives.

. . . Beyond the darkness there is light. Beyond the griefs and pain of the moment is the promise of food and freedom for all in the tomorrows that will come. Beyond the iron bars and barbed wire is the freedom which is our birthright as God's children, which may soon be our gift. Beyond our current distress is the dream of a tapestry through which is woven the rainbow colors of truth, freedom, peace, and love. And in the center of this tapestry is the son of God who became human to uphold the kingdom of justice and righteousness!

Meanwhile let us prepare to celebrate our Christmas. On that day, in the words of the Guatemalan poet Julia Esquivel,

        the word became light
        the word became history
          the word became conflict
            the word became indomitable spirit
            and sowed its seed upon
              the mountains near the river
              and in the valley.
      And those-of-good-will
      heard the angels sing.

Merry Christmas my dear friends!

CHRISTMAS REFLECTIONS

The Christmas story tells us that Joseph and Mary came to Bethlehem to register for the Roman census. Arriving in Bethlehem they found "no room at the inn."

This is the classic story of the plight of the poor throughout history. The decree that forced Mary and Joseph to retreat from Nazareth is today paralleled in the life of the Mindanao peasants forced to leave their lands for strategic hamlets. There is plenty of hotel space in Manila but "no room" for the homeless poor. It is revolting to realize that the price of a room in the Manila Hotel for one night is more than a public school teacher's earnings in a month.

THE POOR MAN

There must have been rooms in the inn. Joseph just didn't have the money or the right connections to get a key to one of those rooms. He was but a poor carpenter and, for the likes of Joseph and Mary, there was only the stable. And God willed the son to be born beyond the tourist belt and the commercial districts and rich conclaves of the elite. God's son was to see the light of day at the periphery of the town, in the decaying inner city, among the scum of the earth, in a shanty that could be demolished any time. God not only became a man; God became a poor man. Jesus had no property, no savings in the bank, no investments in real estate, no diploma, no insurance, nothing.

As John Alexander, coeditor of *The Other Side* wrote, "He was born in a shed to a poor family, in an unimportant, mediocre people. He didn't rule; he served." Jesus knew he could best serve from the position of vulnerability and poverty.

Isn't this the reason religious take the vow of poverty? Why then are some who glory in their vow of poverty so far away from the poor they seek to serve? We grieve to see our church still so rich and privileged, negating the very roots of its Christianity and hindering its prophetic calling.

If God, through the incarnation, categorically manifested a preferential option for the poor, who are we to believe that the kingdom is ours unless we, too, are poor. Being poor means rejecting the insatiable greed of materialism and consumerism. Being poor means looking at social relationships from the perspective of those who are marginalized and utterly dehumanized by oppression and repression. Being poor means to embrace the option of prophets who denounce the evil of injustice and who announce the need to struggle for a just society. Being poor is to insert ourselves in the people's march toward liberation.

Jesus was a poor man and this was his way of life. If we are to be his followers, how can we reject his way of life?

THE POWERLESS MAN

The young courageous girl who became a mother on that Christmas morn had spoken of this in her song: "the Almighty has shown the strength of his arm, he has scattered the proud in their conceit, he has cast down the mighty from their thrones . . . " (Luke 1:51–52). Her son could have been the most powerful king. She, in turn, could have been a president's influential mother. Instead, Jesus was a powerless son of a worker. His birth was an affirmation of God's rejection of greed, absolute power, corruption, the ostentatious display of wealth, the insatiable accumulation of private property, and the use of force to keep the people in subservience. By his birth, Jesus showed us that the real power befitting our dignity as human beings lies in the values of the kingdom. These values run counter to that worldly might that needs wealth, force, status, and influence to keep itself in power.

We've had rich and powerful emperors and kings, but their

empires are gone. None has survived the test of time, and the remains of the empires are locked in museums or sold as commodities in the antique markets. Their followers, servants, and worshipers have long been laid to their rest and they are better left there. Those who thought themselves immortal because they happened to control the destinies of nations and peoples are, like those they ruled, reduced to dust.

> There the wicked cease from troubling,
>> and there the weary are at rest.
> There the prisoners are at ease together;
>> they hear not the voice of the taskmaster [Job 3:17-19].

On the other hand, the child born in the manger, without palace, army, throne, cabinet, or bank account in Switzerland continues to rule. His kingship is in the hearts of believers. His force is in the conviction of followers who are ready to die for their faith, accepting the cost of discipleship willingly. His influence is now and forever in the lives of all those who would commit themselves to the building of a just society where the values of the kingdom have a chance to blossom, like water lilies in a pool which doesn't run dry.

THE HUMAN FACE OF GOD

A detainee can never be the same after his long, indefinite detention. The faces of his fellow detainees will remain engraved in his memory, especially the faces of those who went through hell.

This memory will haunt us in the years to come if we betray our shared dream. There is Pais who lost his sanity because of brutal torture, Juanito who is reduced to a life of pain because of a back broken by torture, Hilda who was raped but whose courage in denouncing her captors is a source of strength to us. Then there is Noli who was salvaged the day after he was taken out of the *bartolina* and the detention center.

These friends remind us of the meaning of courage, and they teach us to triumph over fear. Without the encouraging and challenging words from our codetainees, some of us could not survive this ordeal. We need each other to share pain and agony and moments of joy and jubilation.

Because we are human we need human faces to inspire us, to pull us out of our complacency and our acceptance of the *status quo*.

Jesus is the human face of God's love for us. Born to Joseph and Mary, he has become part of our human race. He, too, was hungry and in need of friendship. He, too, was besieged by all kinds of human problems. He experienced loneliness and betrayal, rejection and harassment. He had doubts, fears, and stage fright. In the last few days of his life he suffered immense pain, collapsed on the streets under the heavy yoke of the cross, and asked for water as he hung dying on that cross. This was prophesied from the time of Isaiah, who saw the Suffering Servant being "arrested and sentenced and led off to die." The face of the crucified Christ is the human face revealing to us God's intervention in salvation history.

That face is all around us today. It is the face of the tribal chieftain who fears that the ancestral land will be lost. It is the face of the peasant's wife who fears that her newly born baby may not live beyond a few months. It is the face of the construction worker who is not sure where his next job is going to be. It is the face of all those whose last flickering hope is that God will not abandon them.

It is the face of a detainee who stares across the blank space ahead, lost in a world of questions. These questions can only be answered by those who have acquired the wisdom from long years of searching for that faith which lifts us out of the narrow limits of our own small space to the stars beyond.

THE DREAM

In the heart of every prisoner of conscience is a dream which refuses to die. Some who could not stand the harrowing ordeal of arrest, torture, and detention may have relinquished this dream, but most find the courage to confront the paralyzing effects of fear. The dream lives on. It is all the detainee has.

The dream is like a tapestry. Woven into it are the outlines of a society characterized by equitable distribution of wealth and by smiling people. Rights are respected and there is no hunger. Gone is the valley of tears. The mountains are green, not bald. The seas are blue, clean, not polluted. The plains are a deep, fertile brown, and not eroded. Children sing songs of life, liberty, and joy.

This, too, is God's dream. Christmas is the rebirth of that dream in Jesus. God became human so that the tapestry could be woven for all of humankind. Years later when Jesus, the itinerant prophet, preached about this dream, multitudes listened and rejoiced. But the mighty and powerful became fearful because of their own narrow dreams, and they became afraid that his dream might come true. They plotted to murder him and succeeded in killing his body. But they could not kill his dream. It has survived the cross and has continued to speak to those who have a feel for life's ultimate meanings.

José F. Lacaba, the poet, wrote about the dream that has made martyrs of many Filipinos who have struggled for the liberation of their oppressed countrymen and women.

> *Sila'y nangarap din nang gising,*
> *subalit ang mga pangarap nila'y*
> *matalim na bituin;*
> *ang mga berdugo't panginoon*
> *ay natakot sa kanilang*
> *mga pangarap,*
> *natakot na baka ang kanilang mga*
> *pangarap ay magkatotoo,*
> *at dahil dito, sila'y wala na*
> *sa ating piling.*

> They also dreamt while awake,
> but their dreams were like
> sharp-bladed stars;
> the cruel masters
> were afraid of
> their dreams;
> they were afraid that
> their dreams might come true,
> and so they are no longer
> in our midst.

This dream, which impelled martyrs, promises to become a reality in the future. Can we not share in this dream for freedom, justice, and peace? For is not their tomorrow our future, and their liberation our redemption?

COURAGE

What made Joseph and Mary courageous? There was nothing extraordinary about this couple, but they were prepared to take risks despite their fears. The child born to them was to become the greatest of all the prophets. He would eventually face his death with the courage of one who trusts totally in God. At an early age he became his own man, able to choose his own destiny. All through his public life he risked, denouncing injustices, naming people for what they were and cursing those who exploited the poor. He chose a collision course with the powers of his time. Many followed him because of his prophetic stand. All this lead to his arrest and ultimate death.

He courageously made his choice and followed it through. When the time came he was ready; the joy of his birth on Christmas was to give way to the sorrow of his death on Good Friday. His mission was fulfilled.

On lonely quiet nights when detainees need inspiration to sustain them, they try to project the future scenario. They believe that one day those who sit on the thrones of this country and their masters in the West, who have subjected the poor to a dehumanized status, will come tumbling down like a deck of cards. One day, the IMF-WB, the TNCs, the international banking system, the CIA and all its local counterparts, the global military complex with its tentacles everywhere, the dictatorships and their cronies, the greedy land-owners and their paid henchmen "will all be cast down from their thrones."

The irruption of the poor in the Third World today foreshadows the coming into reality of the words of Mary in the Magnificat: "The poor will be filled with good things, the rich will be sent away empty." From the dawn of salvation history, God has had a preferential option for the poor. Exodus provides the scenario of God's option for slaves. And the incarnation is the apex of that option.

In the words of Carlos Abesamis, S.J.:

> The child that is born, the son that is given, the baby wrapped in swaddling clothes and lying in a manger is the prophet-healer who will proclaim the kingdom and who will "come"

at the culmination of history to uphold the kingdom of justice and righteousness forevermore, when the fullness of his glory will have filled the earth.

The poor will inherit the earth. They will build the kingdom. They will reject the evil ways of those who opposed the prophets in their midst. They will uphold the biblical tradition of justice and righteousness. And on the Christmas of their liberation, there will be no more tears and fears. There will be food and freedom for all. There will be peace.

May the joy and peace of Christmas be with you and your loved ones.

THE NEW YEAR: 1984

Thank you for your Christmas greetings. I wish I could answer each one who sent the message: "TAKE HEART, DO NOT LOSE HOPE, YOU ARE NOT FORGOTTEN!" Since I cannot answer all, I've prayed for those who reached out, hoping that somehow they'll know how much I have appreciated it.

. . . Throughout the holiday season there was a general air of congeniality, a mood of lightheartedness, and a spirit of kinship. A number of friends who had not previously visited overcame their fear of guardhouses and barbed wire and came to greet us. It was fun to see the reactions of my godchildren as they came to wish their *ninong* a merry Christmas. The visit of countless friends was a highlight, and I am still basking in the warmth of the shared joy at seeing them. The letters from friends afar, of course, were no less reassuring.

But the season was not devoid of fears and tears. Just a few days before Christmas, three young boys were arrested and padlocked here. Nonong, the youngest, is a sixteen-year-old kid who is now facing the charge of subversion. On Christmas Day, the poor kid broke down and cried. However, he soon showed a sense of dignity very few sixteen-year olds possess as he acknowledged this experience to be part of a process of reaching political maturity. On New Year's Eve, George, too, wept bitter tears. Three of his companions in the same subversion case had been released, and he couldn't understand why he would be left behind.

Another dramatic scene unfolded during our Christmas party. The night before, three young men were detained here, suspected members of the underground. The parents were desperate to see them alive, since they were afraid that their sons would be salvaged. The following day a big number of families and friends joined us for our Christmas party. The three were still held incommunicado. The mothers of the three young men managed to sneak into the visitors' area. As we were singing Christmas carols, the mothers were told that they couldn't see their sons. Their plaintive cries drowned the singing and left us stunned. They wailed and the juxtaposition of the mothers' tears with the colorful images of Christmas provided a hard cutting edge to emotions wishing to be lighthearted and carefree.

Despite everything, it was a Christmas full of meaning, and it will be long remembered. My dear friend, the Bishop of Ipil, Monsignor Escaler, wrote me before Christmas and said that it must be quite an experience to spend Christmas in prison as a political detainee, since the setting and the spirit would approximate that of the first Christmas. In a way, I am grateful for the experience. It brought home the meaning of Christmas that can only come from such pain and suffering.

I would like to believe that this experience offers us a guide for the future. At one level, Roy Bourgeois, the Maryknoll priest who is a prisoner of conscience in the U.S. because of his protest against U.S. interference in El Salvador, echoes it well in his words: "I've come to learn that one cannot heal or try to relieve the suffering of others without experiencing and taking on some of the suffering." This is the cost of discipleship.

But we have our share of blessings, too. Those who have tasted the bitterness of life in prison and have agonized through the anger it evokes are also quick to acknowledge the opportunities it offers for growth. These opportunities can come so unexpectedly and in so many different forms. No matter what happens, the hand of God somehow finds its way into our lives.

Now it is 1984. What will this year bring? We shiver at Orwell's vision of 1984. To start the year in prison is definitely Orwellian in character. We are in a situation where Big Brother is closely watching and is trying to reduce us to the status of nonpersons. Perhaps

1984 will not be that tragic. 1983 was bad enough. Could 1984 be worse?

I end this letter with a poem I wrote on New Year's Eve with the wish that 1984 will be a good year for you and all your loved ones.

Old Year/New Year

The old year—
it brought a drought.
Mercilessly the sun
battered emaciated earth.
Fertile land cracked,
widening its yawn to devour
the seeds of life.

The old year—
it brought imprisonment.
Forcefully the captors
ripped apart my being;
flesh and bones shivered,
reduced to a lowly nakedness by
the instruments of terror.

The old year—
it brought a tragedy.
Tempestuously the waves
swallowed friends and boat
as the desolate horizon
provided an opening to
the bowels of death.

The old year—
it brought hunger to malnourished children,
anguish in solitary confinement,
death in its various disguises,
blood on the tarmac,
wasted in a scenario torn apart by
the forces of destruction.

The old year exits;
the new year takes a bow
on the stage where
history will unfold
the collective destiny of a people
outraged to high heaven by
the horror of oppression.

The New Year—
What will it bring?
A flood to ravish the plains?
A multitude of salvaged victims?
An endless flow of tragic events
caused by a darkness that strangles
the promise of a light-filled future?

OR
Is there reason to embrace
the coming of the New Year?
Will green sparkle in the fields?
Will yellow explode in the streets?
Will red deepen the fire of outrage
heightened by the sense of struggle that creates
the upsurge of HOPE?

ASH WEDNESDAY 1984

Salvation history continues to unfold. Recalling the Passion is an attempt to grasp its meaning in the context of our contemporary world.

The historical Jesus was arrested, tortured, and murdered almost two thousand years ago. But in the lives of the people, especially the poor and powerless in the Philippines and in other repressive Third World countries, Jesus continues to experience pain and martyrdom. His body, the collective embodiment of all people, is bruised, abused, trampled upon, and dumped in a shallow grave.

The Filipino religious traditions have highlighted the Holy Week celebrations. The people, especially the peasantry, have a deep devotion to the suffering and crucified Christ, to the consternation of those who would like to see them celebrate the risen Christ more. This religio-cultural phenomenon has been attributed to the people recognizing in the suffering Christ their own experience of oppression and pain. To deepen this recognition may, in turn, challenge us to follow in the footsteps of the Lord who has shown us the ultimate consequence of serving the people!

HOLY WEEK 1984

The Arrest

> *Then the Roman soldiers with their commanding officer and the Jewish guards arrested Jesus, tied him up [John 18:12].*

It was in the dead of night that they came for him. An informer had told them where he was. The arrest was brief.

The Gethsemane scene has been repeated thousands of times in the Philippines since martial law was declared in 1972. There is always something devastating about being arrested. In some cases the person arrested must be resigned to the inevitable—being salvaged—but, even where this does not happen, the fear of it remains. In most cases arrests were made in the dead of night. It may be knocks on the door of a peasant's home at midnight, a military raid of a suspect's house in a city subdivision, or a zoning operation in a squatter area in the city. Alleged "surrenderees" are used as guides.

Accepting the possibility of arrest as a consequence of commitment is essential to the disciple today. The acceptance will not eliminate fear, but it may prevent panic and eventually bring a serenity that can be a source of courage. Being rich and powerful with friends in high places used to provide immunity. No longer. Now distinguished statesmen and women, opposition leaders, bishops, priests, sisters, well-known poets, and social scientists are all included in the list of victims of a regime that must silence any prophetic voice in order to survive. What hope does the poor peasant or worker have?

The Desertion

Then all the disciples left him and ran away [Matt. 26:56].

They had been warned. The disciples had proudly proclaimed that they were ready to stand by him, to be as lambs for the slaughter. But they deserted him immediately.

Yet Jesus would have understood. Peter and the rest of his companions were human, not very different from the ordinary fishers we find in our midst. They have their fears, and repression can paralyze. They have their insecurities, and persecution can make cowards of us all. They have their lives to treasure, families to protect, and interests to safeguard. Human frailty has a way of shredding into pieces the lofty ideals of heart and consciousness.

Throughout history many will desert Jesus when the going gets rough, when the gospel demands a willingness to sacrifice everything including life. Many Christians take pride in their faith when all it demands is a few pieces of silver and some expendable time spent on bended knees begging God's protection for their private property. If blood is smelled along the pilgrim's way, they quickly drop out of the quest for the kingdom and invent their own gods to appease guilt. New forms of idolatry quickly emerge.

Today the challenge for Christians is to withstand the pressure to desert Jesus and to constantly renew their commitment to the gospel option through a deeper involvement in praxis. This demands nothing less than a radical insertion into the lives of the poor and oppressed and a willingness to live the option of building the kingdom at all times.

Many of us are humbled by ordinary peasants and workers, students and tribal leaders who have provided and are providing the living example of people offering their lives that others may live. They know fear, but their love for their brothers and sisters is far stronger than their fear. When for many the final test came, they showed that the demands of a radical discipleship had been internalized. In death, they triumphed over fear!

The Charges

The whole group rose up and took Jesus before Pilate. They began to accuse him, "We caught this man misleading our

people, telling them not to pay taxes to the Emperor and
claiming that he himself is the Messiah, a King." They insisted
even more strongly, "With his teaching he is starting a riot
among the people all through Judea" [Luke 23:1-5].

Brought before the Roman governor, Jesus was confronted by
accusing fingers labeling him a subversive. He was accused of
undermining the only constituted political authority. He was also
accused of political crimes, and there was no way he could untangle
himself from the web of the political conspiracy to get rid of him.

Since the declaration of martial law, the very same charges have
been leveled in the courts against hundreds of suspected subversives throughout the country. Their crimes are against national
security, the definition of which is so nebulous that it is left to those
in power to determine its meaning in the context of any particular
case. As with the gospel account of the trial of Jesus, evidence is
often fabricated, law is manipulated, and witnesses are bought.
Those who work for truth and justice have to be ready to confront
these lies and injustices.

> *Help, Lord. . . .*
> *Every one utters lies to his neighbor;*
> *with flattering lips and a double heart they speak*
> *[Ps. 12:1-2].*

Happy are they who are victims of such lies, for in the end truth
will see the light of day. And in that light those who are persecuted
will behold the source of all truth.

The Collusion of Oppressive Forces

Herod and his soldiers made fun of Jesus and treated him
with contempt; then they put a fine robe on him and sent him
back to Pilate. On that very day Herod and Pilate became
friends; before this they had been enemies [Luke 23:11-12].

The cast of characters involved in the dramatic unfolding of the
last days of the historical Jesus was certainly colorful. They
portrayed not only the class conflict between Jesus and the elite of

Jewish society but also the collusion of the imperialists and local oppressive forces.

Cordial relations did not naturally exist between the imperialists and their Jewish lackeys, but when their interests coincided and had to be protected they had no choice but to close ranks and be allies. Jesus was the victim.

The Filipino people are also caught in a collision course with both the national, privileged elite and its supporters—the government and industrialists of the U.S. The people are the victims and Jesus is once more a victim in them. This collision can be averted only through a radical change of society where the people's interests take priority.

The Cross

> *Then Pilate handed Jesus over to them to be crucified. So they took charge of Jesus. He went out carrying his cross [John 19:16-17].*

In what can only be described as a kangaroo court, Jesus was convicted of alleged crimes. To fulfil his mission of redeeming his people from sin, Jesus offered his life on the cross. He courageously allowed himself to be offered in sacrifice. He has shown us the ultimate expression of holiness, which is also the highest form of manifesting our love for others. No greater love has a person than to offer her or his life for a friend.

The list of our contemporary martyrs continues to expand as the fascist regime continues to devour more victims. Peasants turn up headless in lonely fields. Lay leaders of small Christian communities are salvaged and buried in shallow graves. Village people have been massacred. The bodies of workers who had engaged in organizing laborers are seen floating down rivers. Even priests and professionals have been shot in *conventos,* clinics, and in their homes. Such killings are often reported in the controlled media as the result of encounters between the military and dissidents when in fact they are cases of cold-blooded murder without any encounter.

The crucifixion of our people takes various forms. The nails that pierce their hands and feet are the three basic evils of imperialism, feudalism, and bureaucratic capitalism that are the root causes of our poverty, deprivation, and oppression. As long as these nails remain, our people will be shackled to the cross of despair and powerlessness.

Each one of us at one time or another will be confronted with the reality of our own cross if we genuinely make the gospel a part of our life. When love for the last of one's brothers or sisters is translated into militant commitment for freedom and democracy, justice and peace (and how else can such love be made concrete?), the cross is there. We can only pray that when this moment comes we will have the grace, the courage, and the hope to fully embrace it.

Beyond the Cross

He is not here; he has been raised [Matt. 28:6].

The proclamation of the resurrection shows us the promise of liberation that lies beyond the struggle, beyond the cross. Beyond the pain and suffering is hope. Beyond the blood and tears is joy. Beyond the fear and anguish is life.

Today we are still nailed to the cross. Beyond our cross is the fulfillment of the promise inherent in a people's finally taking its destiny into its own hands. Then the people will be free to sing their own song, to build their dreams, and to worship their God. Their children will no longer fear that men in uniforms will trample on the flowers and grasshoppers in their open fields.

This is the promise of Easter!

Holy Week Celebrated: Creative Liturgy behind Bars

This year we decided to celebrate the Holy Week liturgy creatively. Such celebrations had been denied us in prison; liturgies had become lifeless and spiritless. With Holy Week approaching, we felt it was time to overcome the paralysis of fear and act with some prophetic courage. We also thought that we had to free ourselves from a self-censorship that was becoming more oppressive and far-reaching than the official censorship of the military.

We approached the CO and a minor miracle happened. Our request to prepare the Lenten liturgical celebrations, including a passion play, was granted including permission for two hours' rehearsal daily for ten days. He didn't even ask to see the script. Of course the CO expected a traditional presentation.

Passion plays and liturgical celebrations have become part of our religio-cultural legacy. Most are staged in the traditional style complete with Roman soldiers and the costumes of the time. As detainees, we were naturally drawn to a more contemporary presentation which would portray the suffering, agonizing Christ within the context of present-day agony, suffering, and torture. We also wanted our liturgy to echo what is in the people today—their aspirations for justice and peace, their outrage at violations of human rights, and their commitment to struggle for freedom. How could we meet our own expectations and those of the CO? How could we avoid a clash which would be both controversial as well as explosive? We finally came up with a musical play which would tone down anger and outrage, and we devised the strategy of a play within a play so that the character who portrays Jesus is also a labor organizer in 1984. We decided to cut down on the clenched fists— facial reactions of the guards suggested this—and we simplified and de-emphasized certain scenes so the picket lines didn't have as much fire as real strikes have had.

Rehearsing under the gaze of the soldiers in the guardhouse was, in a way, a blessing as we could tell from their faces when we were going beyond their limits. In the end we struck a fairly good balance because the play remained powerful and acceptable as indicated by feedback from the sympathetic military guards. The military detainees themselves couldn't understand why we were given the CO's permission, for they claim our plays are always "subversive." However, they are the first to reason out that, since we are already in prison, we cannot be arrested anymore!

Casting was easy as we only needed a cast of twenty-five and our "population" of seventy included many talented detainees. In Renato we had a perfect choice for the role of Jesus. He was a worker who, in his own body, had experienced the violence of the military both at picket lines and in the torture room. He could also sing the high notes!

At the outset we agreed that we were going to work collectively, as a community. We wanted to learn together, to criticize each other in the spirit of professionalism, and to encourage each other, particularly in the face of military disapproval and harassment.

Those who have experienced directing amateur theater groups know that one of the hardest things to do is to get the members of the cast to internalize their roles. But experience is the parent of all learning and the spring from which we draw our understanding of life. The detainees had gone through many risks, much pain, anguish, and militancy in their commitment to serve the people. Their discipline and soul-searching hope had been tested both before and after arrest. The director then had so much material to draw from and to work with in the experiences of the detainees.

When the members of the cast had to sing a lament begging God's mercy, they only had to be reminded of their desperate cry to be free in order to capture the intensity of the song. When they acted out their role as workers in a garment factory, they had only to live again the consequences of impoverishment to communicate the tragedy of poverty. When they had to portray the torture of Jesus, they had only to recall the long days and nights of torture that they went through and their body movements eloquently showed the terror of torture. And at Jesus' murder, they remembered all those who had fallen in the pursuit of justice—friends and comrades who have offered their lives for the very same gospel values—and those memories lit fires in their eyes and thunder in their hearts. Pretense was not necessary. They were reliving their own experiences, the price of the commitment which they have willingly embraced.

We also needed to know Jesus, so rehearsals included time for sharing faith. Who was Jesus? What was his class origin? What was his experience of life, of mission? How did he become aware of his mission? What were his hopes, his fears, his insecurities in the face of the growing antagonism to himself and his message? What does incarnation mean today? What is his message? What would his fate be if he lived his prophetic role in the Philippines in the 1980s? Long and interesting were our theological discussions as we tried to understand the deeper meaning of the song lyrics and the symbolic meaning of our movements on stage. "In loving your neighbor and in struggling for justice, you shall be blessed!" was the refrain of the theme song of Jesus which triggered off interesting discussion. Juxtaposing the historical and contemporary Jesus also provoked much enthusiastic discussion, and at one time the military guard on duty shouted: "Why do you insist that Christ was a revolution-ary?"

Through all of this we grew as a community and reached mo-ments of intense pleasure as we saw the exciting fusion of music, poetry, politics, and Christianity.

On Good Friday we had the first two performances in lieu of the reading of the Passion. As I watched the play unfold I reflected on the irony of this presentation. These are men and women who are part of a crowd that the state machinery has labeled as communists and atheists. But as they sing the song about Jesus being the way of truth, justice, and freedom, their clear faith shines through their eyes and only the foolish will not be able to feel its intensity. These are the so-called terrorists with no regard for life and peace, but here they manifest their gentleness and integrity nourished through authentic service to their country. These are the supposed renegades who, it is said, abuse civilians in the countryside, forcing them to submit to their demands. But how evident is their sense of discipline and respect for people's dignity in the way each one contributes to the collective demands of a group not only in presenting a play but also in building a community? These are men and women with deep love for everything that lives.

If the powers-that-be could only remove their blinders they would be able to see people not too different from the apostles with their human strengths and weaknesses. We have to ask ourselves, Who are the believers of today and who are the ones guilty of idolatry?

Easter Sunday 1984

Today we celebrated Easter Sunday. Fortunately, the MetroDis-Com chief was in a mood for celebration so there was no restriction on visitors. Even foreign friends were allowed entry into the stock-ade. A rare, festive atmosphere prevailed.

We gave the final performance of our play and at the end there were tears. Many expressed admiration at the courage and hope of the detainees which truly reflects the timeless message of the resur-rection.

The presentation of *Pasyon 1984* was a breakthrough. Even in the belly of the beast, the spirit lives on to encourage us to preach the good news that we have been called to build the kingdom of truth, freedom, and justice wherever we find ourselves.

As the cast was finishing the last song ("Our pain and suffering is ended at this moment"), I thought: we are now ready to stage the Exodus for our next production!

The play alone would have made our Easter celebration memorable, but after the Mass we had a fiesta. Our relatives brought food and fruit; friends offered Easter eggs and ice cream; and we put on an impromptu program of songs, poems, and games. Most of the visitors stayed for a lunch of *adobo, pancit,* and *dinuguan.* By one o'clock this afternoon the fiesta was over and, once again, we were padlocked.

7

Various Reflections and Challenges

During my interrogation the military angrily asked why bishops, priests, sisters, and layworkers are so committed to justice. We can expect much persecution. KEEP WATCH FOR THE NIGHT OF OUR VIGIL IS LONG.

K. Gaspar

WOMEN

The Women's Association for True Change (WATCH)

Greetings of songs to you all.

. . . 1983 could well mark my awakening to feminism and my denouncement of sexism. I have never belittled women's role, but my concrete experiences this year have underscored the powerful role of women.

In January, at a theological conference in Geneva, I was amazed at the potential and liberating impact of a theology seen from a feminist perspective. In February, at the Popular Theatre Conference in Bangladesh, I marveled at the humanizing impact of the women's concept of popular education, especially juxtaposed against the culture of Bangladesh which seems so suffocating and oppressive for women.

Since March I have been concretely exposed to the courage of women, which has made me realize the importance of supporting efforts to get more women to stand up and be counted in the struggle.

I start with my own mother and my two sisters. The women in our family patiently went through an agonizing vigil when I disappeared. It was they who obtained lawyers, made the supreme court act on my case, and comforted me in prison by just being there, solicitous for my needs. I've come to admire the youngest in our family, Helen, who has shown, despite her age, her frail physical condition, and her own fears and insecurities, her preparedness to move forward and to dare. I have come to see my mother in another light and understood why *Tandang Sora* remains a revered woman.

Then there are my women friends in Manila. In spite of work and family pressures, they supported me and my family and have gone out of their way to look after our needs. They have provided me with the courage to maintain my high spirits, even at times when I thought I would break.

What of the religious women in Davao, in Manila, and abroad? The *"madres"* are of course a legend now, given their involvement in justice and peace. It is the women religious in the Philippines who are giving the Christian faith a credibility it would not have but for their courageous work. In fact, the colonel who was my custodian in Manila said that he looks forward to the day when he can confront the *madres*. Here in the detention center, the word "madre" ranks along with the words *"laya"* and *"dalaw."*

There are also the gutsy women journalists and writers: Arlene Babst, Melinda de Jesús, Monica Feria, Niñez Cacho-Olivares, Sylvia Mayuga, and Christina del Carmen. They are a very significant phenomenon in Philippine media today. These women have consistently shown their commitment to truth and have involved themselves in justice issues despite the censorship and harassment they face. I was lucky that some of them thought I'd make good copy!

Here at the detention center, 95 percent of the visitors are women: mothers, aunts, sisters, nieces. I'll never forget the scene I witnessed just after I was transferred here. A mother was visiting her very young son. Neither said a word. The mother, with tears in her eyes, looked into the eyes of her son while her hand touched his shoulder. The boy looked beyond to the trees and flowers. No word passed between them. But in their looks you could feel the pain, the anguish, the love, the sacrifice, and the hope. This and more had bound them together from his birth. I don't think I'll ever forget that mother's face. No wonder God the Mother created women.

My dear WATCH-ful women friends of Davao, how can I ever say thank you for your help, support, prayers, concern?

Columban Sisters

I join you in spirit and in prayer as you gather for your assembly. You meet against a backdrop of crisis, increasing dissent, and outrage from our people. In the face of this crisis, the bishops have strongly proposed that "we need to revamp our entire economic and political structure to make it more responsive . . . to the ends of life." How are we to share in this gigantic task? This surely is the key area for your consideration. What to me is most important at this stage is not so much the concrete and specific strategies that will be employed but rather the general orientation and attitude we need at this stage.

Wherever you are working and whatever your ministry—schools, health, justice and peace, tribal Filipinos, pastoral work—there is need to embody an orientation where faith is integrated with life. This provides the anchor for our commitment to life and asks of us a basic compassion for the disadvantaged and marginalized. Opening our hearts to them, we enter into the same covenant that God has made with the people of God as they seek liberation from all that dehumanizes them.

Segundo Galilea in *Mission in the Gospel* has written that "the principal motivation of the missionary is mercy. This love is a love which wants to be effective, which wants to change things, which wants to help all others free themselves of their miseries of all kinds. . . . Mercy is essential to the spirituality of mission." Women do have the inherent quality of being compassionate and merciful. Someone said that women are more drawn to be in solidarity with those who are oppressed because women have always been oppressed. They have always shared the fate of being pushed to the periphery! Being women religious, you have this gift of mercy as well as your vocation to serve the people as the necessary framework to incarnate yourselves in the lives of the people in our society today. You have what it takes; all that is needed is to nourish your gifts further and to situate them within the mainstream of the people's struggle for liberation.

. . . In the wake of the Aquino assassination the members of the middle class have become increasingly aware and militant in their commitment to justice. These are the people with whom you are working in the schools. They are also the ones most unconscienticized and indifferent to the need for change. Here lies your opportunity to be part of the movement for conscienticizing the middle class. How this can be done in a more systematic manner is the challenge to Catholic schools in the Philippines today. There is need for an alternative education more relevant to the times and for our schools to really become channels of evangelization and not cultural institutions reinforcing the oppressive *status quo*.

Those working in other ministries also face this challenge, although the praxis may not be as difficult. Whatever our ministry is, it is essential that we develop mechanisms of mutual support. We no longer can afford to allow those in traditional ministries to be alienated from those pioneering in new ministries and vice versa. The times call for a multisectoral approach to liberation.

. . . Please join me in praying that I may soon be set free along with all the political prisoners in the Philippines.

Maryknoll Sisters

You are a missionary congregation. You have come to witness to God's loving presence among the people. In the course of your immersion in our people's lives you have rediscovered God as the vulnerable and manipulated victim of the privileged elite. You have seen God's face in the weather-beaten faces of the downtrodden who cry out for justice. You hear God's voice calling out for help because the people can no longer carry the heavy burden of slavery in the land meant for the brave and free! You, then, came to realize that the people themselves are the ones offering you the nourishing and purifying gift of God's love. Behind those sad and haunting eyes is a spark that breaks out occasionally in bright smiles which mirror all the hopes sown in the hearts of those who fully trust in God's mercy and compassion. You also then begin to realize that missionary work is urgently needed back home, in the very belly of the beast, where decisions are made and policies set up which have torturous implications for millions of people in the Third World.

But this moment of awakening brings conflict in you. Even as you resolve it temporarily within yourself, you are confronted with violent reactions from family and friends who do not see the international capitalist order from the point of view of the least of our sisters and brothers. How much hate mail has Maryknoll, New York, received from across the U.S. denouncing your liberation thrust? I remember sitting down with Brother Ray in his office at the Maryknoll house in Philadelphia in the summer of 1981 and reading through the hate letters. It wasn't easy reading. The letters brought pain and a sense of frustration. But you have to face that reality back home and accept the conflict that is arising as you live out a prophetic role in your own country.

Those who love with the passion of saints and martyrs cannot avoid conflict and tensions. Precisely because they love their fellow human beings they will antagonize the few who have nothing but hatred in their hearts. It is ironic that those who challenge others to love the people provoke in a few such hatred and murder. The lives of Jesus himself, John the Baptist, the apostles, Gandhi, Martin Luther King, Archbishop Romero, the four American church-women, Victor Jara, and Macliing Dulag, among many others, are symbolic of this contradiction.

We are called to praise God in the beauty of creation. We are destined to live in harmony with the mountain streams and wild-flowers as well as with the birds and carabao. We are meant to embrace each other as we seek the goodness in each other's heart. We are called to build communities and a family of nations that will acknowledge the Motherhood and Fatherhood of a just, righteous, loving, and compassionate God. We cannot allow ourselves to become perpetrators of greed and hatred. We should be a song that drives away antagonism, a bridge that brings people of goodwill together, a tree that provides the comforting shade under which others can gather to celebrate their brotherhood and sisterhood.

Wherever we are we must be committed to justice and peace. We must work to establish solidarity among the family of nations so that there will no longer be any more superpowers to kick the weak ones around. We must strive for a just international order where all nations have equal access to the goods of the earth. When we are part of this struggle and dream we can sing:

Love and faithfulness will meet;
justice and peace will embrace.
Humility's loyalty will reach up from the earth,
and God's justice will look down from heaven
[Ps. 85:11–13].

You are part of a congregation that lays claim to a history of establishing new frontiers of mission work. You can be justifiably proud of that fact, which remains a living reality. Despite your limitations and insecurities you have forged a solid sense of purpose and have gone ahead charting new frontiers based on your discernment of the signs of the times in this country.

As I end this letter, I glance at the Maryknoll Sisters' ring that I wear on my ring finger. Among the images and symbols I see is a six-petaled flower. I offer you this flower as a symbol of my deep affection and a prayer that you may have an enjoyable and fruitful assembly. Warmest greetings to all of you and also to Father Ralph Salazar and Bishop Labayen. Take care.

The Sisters of the Rural Missionaries, Mindanao

A solitary candle burns brightly on my table as I write you this letter from our prison cell. We have had sporadic brownouts these past few days. Is this some form of economic sabotage?

Despite the inconvenience, I welcome the brownout. Given the times, there is something very symbolic about being enveloped by darkness. The sight of a flickering candle is reassuring and provides warmth, especially as it reminds me of those who give light and allow themselves to be consumed while offering themselves wholeheartedly. I think of all of you because you have been like the proverbial candle. You have been shedding light both on our beleaguered society and divided church.

It is good to know that nine more sisters joined you in your recent meeting and made their commitment during the Mass. Congratulations! As long as new members embrace the R.M. mission there is the assurance that your pioneering efforts in new ministries will continue. Are you serious about recruiting priests to join you? This would be an interesting development which should provide further strength and variety to your group. Given our present situation, the need to have more in the field at the side of the people is urgent. This is especially true for courageous and committed rural missionaries, since the concentration of problems will remain in the turbulent countryside of Mindanao.

You hold the distinction of being pioneers in new ministries in the 1970s. Yours is a legacy which is going to stay forever in the minds of all those who will follow your pioneering prophetic spirit! You made the jump from secure and comfortable convent walls into the nitty-gritty world of the marginalized and discovered that the gospel could only be translated into praxis by dismantling all the prefabricated mission approaches which only reinforce oppression. In that discovery you evolved new ministries.

Recently, one of these ministries, the community-based health program, was labeled a subversive front by the government's propaganda machine on the front pages of major national newspapers. It is tragic that we have reached the stage where this ministry of healing, which serves a very concrete and neglected need of the poor, is considered dangerous by the state. It is so ironic that the government—which has spent millions of pesos to duplicate the program of barefoot doctors and has failed dismally—would crush a program that has shown its effectiveness in enabling the poor to handle their own health needs. Instead of supporting this program, the government is now determined to suppress it by declaring it subversive in character. Consequently, anyone in the barrio who knows how to do acupressure or acupuncture will run the risk of being arrested. Those who cultivate herbal gardens will draw suspicion. It sounds so absurd, but then a situation of war is always tragically absurd!

The more you are identified by your preferential option for the poor, the more vulnerable you will become. In the context of this vulnerability and powerlessness, anything can happen to you. Consider the four U.S. women missionaries who were killed by the right-wing death squads of El Salvador in December 1980. They were involved in the classic corporal works of mercy of feeding the hungry and sheltering the homeless. But in serving these refugees, their work was considered "political" by the sinister, powerful right-wing forces who plotted to get rid of them for good. Despite the protection provided by their government and church, they were powerless to resist the onslaught of institutionalized violence. They were vulnerable unto death.

I'm sure your faith-life reflections, especially among the people, confront these truths. When we are most vulnerable the Lord's counsel and compassion become so real. Moments of pain and suffering are also our moments of grace. These can be the moments when we are most united in Christ!

Another historical fact is that you have smashed the myth that you are just a group of highly motivated but naive religious who have allegedly allowed themselves to be manipulated by supposedly cunning infiltrators. Your witness is now shared by many sisters. Like your counterparts in the urban areas, you have made your presence felt in the front lines of the protest movement. Together you have shown that the women religious of this country are capable of great courage. You have become a symbol of our women who are defying the male-dominated power structure and are demanding a radical restructuring of society. You have made it known to our people that there are church workers who are witnessing to the gospel and championing the God-given rights of the poor as an integral part of their vocation.

If this is my lucky year I will be with you at your next general assembly and we can once more sing our songs together.

There goes the candle!

FILIPINO LAY MISSIONARIES

I was glad to know that you came together last July for your meeting. I can imagine that you had very rich sharings and discussions on your vocation and its challenges and frustrations in the context of our country's crisis.

. . . To choose the struggle of the poor has become an integral aspect of our option. Have you shared on the question of what precisely is the expression of the poor's struggle at this crossroads of our country's history? There is an urgency in seeking the answer to that question because so many of our brothers and sisters are agonizing, suffering, and dying.

The greater part of the answer can, perhaps, be discerned from the signs of the times as interpreted by the poor themselves inspired by the Spirit's force. Even without clear manifestations of the "faith aspect," we have to believe in the power of the Spirit who has always intervened in history to bring the people closer to their dream of liberation. With or without the church, the people will make historical choices. It will be to our credit as Christians if we can continue to be present to this creative process and to offer our contribution to the full humanization of the politicized poor.

Wherever we are we must be in constant dialogue with them to avoid building ghettos in the belief that we effect change in society solely through "the heart's transformation." Look around you. There are many doors that could be opened to bring you into a new understanding of the basis of social unrest. Trust the people. They have opened the door. Have you entered?

Above all, I want to say: CONTINUE. You know what awaits you, so when it comes, trust in the Lord, trust our people, and trust yourselves.

THE SEMINARIANS OF ST. MARY'S THEOLOGATE

Thank you all for your prayers and kind words. I am very privileged to have friends like you who provide me with much needed encouragement.

. . . Today is my last day in court. I pray that none of you will ever have to go through the anguish of arrest and detention but, at this time of our country's history, anyone who takes the gospel seriously may become a victim of the state's repression. Because of this I am happy that the bishops responsible for your seminary have held on to the vision of a formation attuned to the needs of the local church—a church struggling to be actively involved in the task of social transformation. Seminary formation today cannot afford to alienate seminarians from their class origins, but must rather enrich their appreciation of gospel values and their acceptance of the imperative option for the poor.

. . . Soon you will finally be with the people. What do the next few years hold? . . . Social unrest is intensifying in the countryside, and this, in turn, has led to the escalation of militarization. As institutionalized violence increases, the people turn even more against the regime. The cycle goes round and round with more and more bloodshed and more and more crying widows and orphans. How will you respond as pastors?

The answer, I hope, has been the subject of your many reflections, class deliberations, and liturgical celebrations. The same answer must have been evoked when you went to listen to the peasants as they expressed their honest expectations of their pastors. Perhaps you have already made your own commitment as the Spirit has led you to an option. Whatever the answer, I trust that it has come or will come as a grace from the Lord of history, coinciding with the people's own historical quest for the kingdom.

COLUMBAN FATHERS

It is fortunate that the whole force of the case against the Negros Nine [see also pp. 26–29 and 66–68 above] has been dismissed by the government. The prosecution's position, having been built on fabrications and lies, could not withstand the pressure of truth and solidarity. It finally collapsed, vindicating the prophets who certainly were an inspiration to us political prisoners here in Davao.

Part of the "blessing" of their incarceration was the fact that their witness demythologized the government's claim that there has been no systematic persecution of the church, but only of "infiltrators." The Negros Nine's insistence that they were arrested, detained, and charged with murder because of their involvement with justice issues through the BCCs, helped to crystallize the consequences of our option for the poor in our given situation.

The case also exposed the moral bankruptcy of this regime. If an Australian and an Irish Columban, backed up by their powerful bishop, superiors, and embassy officials, could be arrested and detained, who is safe from the regime's absolute powers? Their arrest also showed the collusion between the military and the sugar barons of the Negros establishment. You step on the toes of the rich and they won't let you get away with it.

. . . The ones who are most vulnerable are the poor themselves. Of the Negros Nine, the six laymen are the most powerless, and Niall and Brian would be the first to acknowledge it. The Columbans and other religious have shown concern about what could eventually happen to the six laymen. There is reason for that concern because, after their celebrated case, no one can guarantee

them safety either in the short or long term. We can only hope that
protection is given, no matter how inadequate.

. . . The odyssey of the Negros Nine must have been as agonizing to all of you as it was to your brother Columbans. It must also
have provided you the rare chance to individually and collectively
look into the Columban presence in the Philippines and to discern
where you are in regard to your evangelization work among the
people. Like the Jesuits, the men of the Pontifical Institute for
Foreign Missions (P.I.M.E.), the Maryknollers, and members of
other congregations who have experienced state persecution, you
must have felt the pressure and wondered why this happened to
your men. Given the involvement of your brothers in a variety of
ministries, including justice and peace, it is no wonder that the
Negros Nine phenomenon did erupt. After all, Negros has always
been explosive, and the church's presence there has not always
provided comfort to the rich and powerful!

It is possible that after the experience of the Negros Nine you, as
a group, will take an ever stronger prophetic stance inspired by the
same Spirit who has always provided strength to those who would
preach the good news to the poor. But it is possible that some may
become more concerned about being "prudent" and take the "safe
path," either consciously or unconsciously.

. . . It is not easy for everyone to be comfortable in being
identified with the militant church or with the demands of taking a
definite pro-people position in regard to justice and peace issues. I
guess that is a given reality that must be acknowledged at all times.
We can only respect each other's options and choices; after all, no
one can claim to have a monopoly of the stirrings of the Spirit. Still,
there is need to face up to the issues because of the demands of the
restless times.

More and more, an agenda is being articulated by the local
church. If the local church is to be truly incarnated in the lives of
poor peasants, workers, fisherfolk and tribal communities, they
must articulate the agenda. And this agenda has become more and
more anchored in the historical need of the church to accompany
the people in their march toward liberation.

. . . The foreign missionaries are asked to integrate themselves
into the people's history, culture, life realities, faith dynamics, and
their emerging spirituality/theology/national identity. To refuse to

enter into the people's hearts and their total being is to refuse to acknowledge the rights of the hosts to determine what the guests' role is to be in their household.

Nationalism is in our soul, and like the protagonist in Leon Uris's *Trinity,* we can also say: "There is no mystery more intense than a man's love for his country. It is the most terrible beauty of all."

We are grateful that you are with our people, who have nothing but appreciation for your missionary zeal. We ask you to share in our struggles, pains, hopes, and dreams, not only on a theoretical level, but also in praxis. Most of you have gone through your own struggle on how best to express your solidarity with our people. This may become even more intense as the situation continues to deteriorate. If you remain truly in dialogue with the poor and powerless, especially those who are politicized and have made their faith option despite the risks, it will not be difficult to find your place. We have to trust the people. They are the ones God will fill with good things even as God sends the rich and powerful away empty.

I also write to thank you for your generous support since I was arrested and subsequently detained. I have received letters from many of you in Ireland and Australia and even Pakistan.

If I am acquitted, I will see you soon. If not, I will see you later!

BISHOPS

[Aug. 1984] The present reign of terror and death in this country was the theme of the most recent joint pastoral letter of the Catholic Bishops Conference of the Philippines (CBCP). Entitled "Let There Be Life" it took up the defense of the sacredness of human life. It is to the credit of the bishops that they have come out with a prophetic statement, the message of which was predictably repudiated by the regime which denounced the church's interference in political affairs.

The bluntness and preciseness of some statements in the letter reveal a significant shift in the bishops' perception of current realities. "For years now we have been . . . in a state of war," is clearly an acceptance of the intensity of the social conflict raging throughout the country. Their reading of the political economy, "political problems will intensify . . . we must have enough of fear, even *now* . . . the economy is in shambles . . . the spector of hunger . . . the present outlook is bleak and the future even bleaker," deviates from the whitewashing of the regime and echoes the feelings of the people, both the political and the apolitical. The bishops claim that we are now faced "with the reality of death." What is the Christian response in this situation? The bishops start out with a militant position: "we need to revamp our entire economic and political structure to make it more responsive than it presently is to the ends of life." This will be accomplished through non-violence, they insist, through "working constantly, strenuously for justice that refuses adamantly to destroy life for the cause of justice itself."

These are beautiful words, and, if concretized in actual justice and peace programs at the diocesan and parish levels, would go a long way in the defense of life. The bishops have never been wanting in articulating the social message of the Gospel, but for a number of them, the words have not taken on flesh. They call for "great acts of self-sacrifice," in today's crisis. The people, especially among the harassed and battered villages where there are Basic Christian Communities, have been offering their lives. What greater acts of self-sacrifice can we still ask from those whose faith now compels them to shed their blood so that others may live? We look at our church leaders and ourselves, churchworkers, and what have we to offer apart from words? We have a long way to go before we have the authenticity of our BCC leaders.

"Let There Be Life" though, is a significant move from the CBCP and we can thank the Spirit for evoking it.

It is imperative that the Church should, once and for all, rid its consciousness of the influence of the ideology of the national security. It cannot afford to be paralyzed by the fear of "being infiltrated and manipulated." The myth that there is a communist behind every confessional box and convent post has to be crushed. We cannot forever insist on being pure and not tainted by anything red before we move an inch. We do not have a monopoly of a "purely Christian motive" as the point of departure for an active involvement in justice. We rush to our neighbors because they need help. When we see no distinction between Christian and human, no dichotomy between political and spiritual, no rift between God's saving grace and historical options, we will be better prepared to truly defend life.

SCHOOLS

The Challenge to HCCD on Its Silver Anniversary

There is a need to remember the context in which your school exists. It cannot insist on being an island surrounded by a body of water now turning red with the blood caused by the institutionalized violence of the repressive regime. It cannot remain a ghetto, safe in itself and without any compassion for the marginalized sectors of society. It cannot be an ivory tower, pretending that all is well when, in fact, there is a state of siege and the people's cry of outrage is deafening.

How long do you think you can ignore the salvagings, the human rights violations, the insurgency, and the economic crisis and its devastating impact on the lives of the poor? Do you believe that you are a boat that can always safely weather the choppy waters during a stormy night?

Something very historical will happen in the next twenty-five years. It could involve the radical transformation of Philippine society. Already the process that could lead to such an eventuality has begun. Can you not see the signs? What are you doing to prepare for the major shift that will occur to change the course of history?

All I have for you are questions. If you ask me what needs to be done, I will throw it back to you. You have the wisdom to find the answers, but you must first accept the questions as valid. If the school is to be relevant now and in the next few years, it has to wake up and seek the light.

He reflects on the significance of the symbols associated with this school:

. . . The cross is the symbol of God's salvific plan for God's children. Through his cross, Jesus paid the price for his identification with the poor and downtrodden. Today, the people bear the cross of oppression and dehumanization. Are you going to embrace this same cross and be in solidarity with the poor?

The heart is the symbol of Christ's love and compassion for the least of humankind. His heart went out to the widows and orphans, the prostitutes and fisherfolk, the lowly and scum of the earth, and the victims of the abuse of those in power. His call to service that came from this heart was for the preaching of the good news to the poor, for bringing sight to the blind, liberty to the captives, and freedom to the oppressed. He encouraged us to open our hearts to our neighbor in need. Today these neighbors are the salvaged victims, those abused by the military, those who are driven away from their farms and forced into hamlets, the workers laid off from their jobs, the malnourished children, and all those whose lives do not reflect their God-given dignity.

Is your institution, now in its twenty-fifth year, imbued with the Spirit of Jesus? Or is it but an extension of the spirit of capitalism, materialism, and consumerism which perpetuates the *status quo*?

I had better close now, or my questions will never end!

Ateneo de Davao

We were watching the news on television and suddenly you [a Jesuit priest] were there with the U.S. ambassador. The newscast showed us the blessing of the university wing and we learned about the "warm" reception that the ambassador received during his visit to the city, including the rally. . . . I felt very uneasy about his presence on the campus and found his coming to grace the affair very objectionable. Of course I have nothing against him personally, and I am sure he couldn't care less about my opinion of him. It is what he represents that I, and a growing number of Filipinos, find so offensive. In a Third World country like the Philippines, where U.S. neocolonial policies have stunted economic growth and have spurred the rise of a repressive dictatorship, he represents U.S. imperialism. Even the moderate and formally apolitical middle-class sector of our society now joins in the battle cry "Dismantle the U.S.-Marcos dictatorship!" We must be concerned with this issue and do something about it. The manifestations of Washington's blatant interference in our internal affairs are everywhere. There is the dictatorship itself, which could not have lasted all these tragic years if it had not been for Washington's support. There is the huge defense budget which could have been inflated and supported only by Washington's military-aid program which, in turn, has been used to suppress legitimate dissent and the escalating resistance. There is the design to make our economy perpetually backward industrially and primitive technologically. There is the pressure to open our markets to free trade in order to ensure protection to transnational corporations, provide supplementary local capital to foreign investments, and lower tariff walls.

Such interference has spawned the rise of neocolonialism which makes a mockery of our so-called independence and sovereignty. We don't have to possess the genius of a Claro M. Recto or a Renato Constantino to understand the nefarious impact of being held captive by an aggressive superpower. Through its nonnegotiable stand on the strategically crucial military bases and the protection of American investments in this part of the world, Washington has assisted a fascist regime characterized by greed, corruption, and abuse of power. U.S. policy in this country has led to the setting up of this puppet regime, the reign of which has led to terror and death.

. . . The Ateneo, and naturally the Jesuits, are very explicit about forming their students to be men and women *for* others. I believe we need, also, to be formed to be *against* those who dehumanize "the others." U.S. imperialism is dehumanizing. It prevents the people in poor countries from being fully human. It assists in trampling down the God-given dignity of the marginalized. It follows that we must seek to cut its tentacles, even if in the process we get hurt.

It is never easy for me to sound militant because I fear being misunderstood. My sixteen months' experience as a prisoner of conscience has, at times, made me quite hesitant to speak out my "radical thoughts." I keep fighting this fear which is an agonizing process. There is always the temptation to succumb to the culture of silence in order to appease the powers that be.

But, in the words of Martin Luther King, "Today we cannot afford to be silent. Without provocation we must speak out without fear, we must bring out the truth. Without hope we will be strangled. But with the courage and confidence in truth and justice we shall overcome."

Shalom!

MINDANAO CHURCH

Quo vadis, Mindanao Church? Where are you going? What is at the end of the road? Perhaps, like Christ, you will reach the hill. Perhaps you too will be crucified. Fear not. The cross reaches up to the heavens but it also reaches out to the people. The Lord will declare a new history for your people. It is the history of your people's liberation. It is the destiny of a people offering themselves for their prophetic option.

TROCAIRE (IRISH BISHOPS' AGENCY FOR THIRD WORLD DEVELOPMENT)

[May 13, 1983] I am writing this letter from our cell here at the detention center on this forty-ninth day of my detention. I hope it reaches you in time for TROCAIRE's tenth anniversary. Greetings of peace and may the Spirit of justice and love be in your midst!

As you know I was invited by TROCAIRE to join you in the celebration, and I had accepted the invitation. At the time of my arrest I was carrying materials which I had collected to help me write my speech. Because of my arrest on March 26, the speech was never written.

. . . I wrote earlier saying that only a miracle could get me out of prison before the second week of June. Not that I don't believe in miracles (my having stayed alive is a small miracle in itself), but the implications of a PCO make me quite realistic. Besides, the angels that set St. Peter and his companions free from their prison seem to have lost their jobs!

I pray for the success of TROCAIRE's tenth anniversary. For me there is only one indicator of success: that TROCAIRE remains steadfast in its preferential option for the poor and oppressed and deepens its commitment to serve the lowly and downtrodden. I pray that all of you, linked in one way or another to TROCAIRE and its concretization of the gospel, may always have the strength to move on in spite of the risks, difficulties, frustrations, and sleepless nights. To witness to the gospel sounds very easy, but we all realize the weight of the burden. To follow Christ is a challenge we encounter every now and then, but we know that the price of discipleship is not a joke. Even if we are so sure that we have taken the option embodied in Luke 4:18–19, the temptation to drop it is always there.

To be a Good Samaritan in our society today is to take the option for the poor lying almost dead on the street, perhaps dumped there by death squads. We have to be ready to change the agenda of our lives and give up our passivity. To be a Good Samaritan no longer means just being inconvenienced by taking the injured person to a hospital and paying the bills. It now involves an openness to understand why the person got into the situation in the first place and the willingness to take a risk in case the person is declared "subversive." To be a Good Samaritan, we not only literally carry the needy person on our back to a place of comfort and safety, but we also carry the responsibility of seeing to it that justice be given this person.

. . . A preferential commitment to the poor demands that we read the signs of the times from the perspective of the poor and not from our petty bourgeois framework. How do the peasants whose children are malnourished because of centuries of landlessness understand the reason behind their deprivation? How do workers living in urban slum areas, surviving on unjust wages because strikes are prohibited, explain the cause of their oppression? How do the mothers of both the rural and urban poor, faced with the constant threat of hunger and hopelessness for the future of their children, see their desperate situation?

We have to listen to their voices. We have to force ourselves to listen to their reading of their own situation and to try to understand how they want to change their dehumanizing status. The conscienticized and politicized poor can teach us the way to a just and humane society if we are only willing to acknowledge that they are the ones to shape their own destiny!

Life as a political prisoner is full of fear, agony, and anxiety. It has its blessings, though, and in a way it is a "gift" from God if one can survive it. The enrichment of one's faith comes about with the long hours of dialogue with God. Francis of Assisi's prayer is a challenge ("that I may console rather than seek to be consoled . . .") in a situation where other detainees have to be comforted because they have just been to hell.

I end this rather long letter with a prayer—that all of us, in whatever way we can, will continue to show *Trocaire* [mercy] and to serve the poor and oppressed!

THE LEGACY TO FUTURE GENERATIONS

This week I got a letter from Alice in the ASI. She mentioned her difficulty in explaining to her son, my godchild, Ed Karl, why I am in prison and what a political detainee is. It is the same problem Clement and Nancy had when they brought their son Pierre to visit me in prison. Both are five-year-old kids. How do you explain these realities to innocent children? Yet it is for them that we are willing to take risks and face sacrifices. Without the Ed Karls, Bayanis, Tom-Toms, Jamads, Malayas and Al Kris Davids, we would not bother to look forward to a just and humane society. The struggle will be protracted, and it may still take a long time before social transformation reaches fruition in this society. As we approach middle age we accept that it is not we who are to enjoy the gains of a victorious struggle. It is the generation of Bayani and Malaya that hopefully will harvest the fruits. Meanwhile, we rage and take our position beside the people as they advance on their pilgrimage and, with hope, we look forward to the dawning of that new day. Bert had this to say at MSPC #5: "As the Exodus event took place after God saw the people's affliction and heard their cry, so may the people's cries today storm the heavens and may Yahweh, who is dwelling among his people, rise up with them to the heights of a new heaven and a new earth."

We always knew it would take time, and my detention has deepened this conviction. I realize how parallel is the praxis of our "indefinite" detention as detainees and the "indefinite" duration of the people's own struggle. But despite this conviction, the frustration remains. Freedom, when will it come? Tomorrow? Next month? In ten years? In twenty years? It is like being kidnapped and hijacked with no idea of when or how the ordeal will end. Prisoners in the city jail with a definite sentence are to be envied!

What has helped? Recently I read a quote from Francis Moore Lappe in an AWD newsletter where she said: "We need to develop a perspective longer than a lifetime. . . . Seeing ourselves as part of a historical process longer than our [own] life's process can be a source of courage." I now realize the importance of this "long-term perspective" both in regard to my detention and my freedom, as well as to the people's struggle and their eventual victory. It is in this context that the young of today provide us with inspiration. They may not understand anything that is happening. But, as I told Alice, I look forward to the year 1995 when Ed Karl will be seventeen and I can explain things to him. Perhaps he will understand. Wouldn't it be something if our godchildren could be proud of us and our generation! We would have shared with them the meaning of life. And what else is the role of a godparent?

CHALLENGES

Personal

Challenges are all around us. We prisoners are made to bow our heads in front of the military authorities, but I refuse to allow them to dehumanize me. This has angered them, but I am still in one piece despite their harassment and punishment. They must find me too belligerent, but I will denounce their abuses and demand our rights even if they put me into a *bartolina*. Even a hunger strike becomes a matter of practice. After our experience I appreciate better the Christian tradition of fasting. Previously, it was only explained to us in terms of an individual piety. After this I may, like Nena, be ready for a monastic life. Our life has similarities with the life of monks. I sometimes even fantasize I'm in a Trappist monastery.

Challenge to Change

We can never be the same after serving time in prison. We have to change, to become more of a person; otherwise, the brutality and frustration of the ordeal will diminish us as human beings. This is the challenge for all detainees, and the quality of our communal interaction is determined by our mutual desire to enable each one to grow and develop.

One area of change is in the sharpening of sensitivity. Existence is so confined that detainees become very perceptive with regard to what happens with their confined space. They have a heightened awareness of the vibrations and undercurrents that exist in their surroundings and of the impact of dislocation, alienation, and loneliness that is part and parcel of prison life.

On the one hand, it is easy to perceive the negative consequences of heightened sensibilities. We are not in the company of saints whose patience stretches to the sky, so violent words and fists fly all over the place. Small problems become major ones as arguments are put forward, and heated discussions can quickly turn into bloody confrontations. Sometimes I get the impression that problems are created for the sole reason of maintaining dramatic overtones so that the days don't become dull and uneventful!

On the other hand, there are positive aspects of a sensitivity that intensifies with imprisonment. We become more perceptive to what goes on in the hearts and minds of our codetainees, to the signals which evoke our compassion. We become better able to control tempers or shrug off impatience, and in this way irritants that sow discord are minimized. There is growth in consideration and appreciation for family and friends, and we find ourselves better able to express love in response to their generosity and concern. We gradually become closer to nature, more observant of the change of seasons; we become more aware of where the wind is blowing, what cloud patterns are formed before a heavy downpour, where there is good soil for flower pots, and when to expect the shrill sounds of cicadas greeting the coming of warmer days in late March.

There is then our growth in sensitivity to the realm of meaning and symbol. It shows in the art produced in detention centers and in the choice of songs for liturgical celebrations. It is seen in the lifestyle that detainees assume, a lifestyle close to that of the masses. In fact, we find comfort in being able to share the actual poverty, deprivation, and oppression of the majority of the people.

Prison also gives us the luxury of time to reflect on life's meaning, on where we came from and where we are going. When we ask what brought us to this prison we are reminded of the significance of the options we have taken. Our previous search for meaning in our lives has led us to this. Reflecting in this way helps prepare us for any tragic consequences that may be the result of the choices we have made.

CONTEMPORARY SPIRITUALITY

Grace

Can grace spring from the political detainees' collective agony and be offered for the good of those who need it most? Does God look kindly on our sacrifice and transform our fears into courage, our anger into hope, our doubts into clear visions so that we will not falter as we march toward our dream? Are we bearers of the legacy left by the prophets of old who were persecuted for their uncompromising stand for truth and justice? Is our witness of any value in terms of the kingdom, even as the kingdom is still so many lifetimes from where we find ourselves today? As we search for answers, we know that the Lord will show us the way.

. . . What is essential is that we understand imprisonment as an integral consequence of commitment. Without this, detainees just become angry and bitter and are not able to grasp the meaning of their present tribulation. This meaning lies in their love for God, for country, and for the people. On the one hand, no sacrifice is too small or insignificant and, on the other hand, the offering of life itself is not too great. Above all is the desire to witness to the establishment of a just society which is a foreshadowing of the kingdom; for integral to salvation history is the people's historical struggle for liberation.

To be liberated, to be free—these are the thoughts that carry one through the days of anguish, the nights of rage!

As long as detainees assert their rights and deepen their commitment to serve the people, they remain free. The powers-that-be can only physically imprison the body. They can never imprison persons' total being, especially that part of them that dreams. Detainees can remain free within prison walls if they can still raise their minds and hearts to the infinite space above. There they can hope and dream for the day when the boundary of their lives will no longer be the barbed wire that encircles the detention center but the very spheres of the earth. They can claim to be as free as the birds because they can still look up to the heavens and pray even as they seek to resign themselves to God's will.

As long as detainees can sing a haunting song to break the stillness of the nights, a song of deliverance that lifts the hearts of their companions, the bell of freedom rings. As long as detainees can bring their hands to embroider the image of a bird that dares to break free from a cage, they express their indomitable will to struggle. And as long as they can plant a seed that will one day be a flower, they know that captivity will never hold them.

What is the secret? Is it grace? Perhaps it is. I refer to grace understood in the totality of its meaning. This is the grace that has enabled us to grow through the years. It is the grace that has led us to a deepened solidarity with the poor, those poor whose wisdom and courage have continually humbled us. We have received this grace through the fisherfolk and farmers in Mati and Bato-bato and the workers in Davao and Butuan; they have shown us what following the gospel is all about. We have been touched and converted by their genuine witnessing. This is the grace that leads to an involvement in the struggle for justice, which opens us up to accept the cost of discipleship and the risks involved, and to be prepared to be "handed over" when the time comes.

Ultimately, this grace is the gift of God who blesses us with fatherly/motherly love. Only through the totality of this gift of grace have I been able to survive as I have until now. I am very fortunate to have friends who continue to pray for me and who ask other people to include me in their prayer. Tom O'Brien wrote recently that he attended a liturgy at a priory in Vermont and, during the canon of the Mass, heard the monks mention my name. Apparently I am one of those for whom they are praying.

It is never easy to keep on trusting God. In the earlier stage of my detention, I would nag God every day to get me released. And when night came and I was still in prison I used to feel so rejected. Slowly, painfully, I realized that I had never really trusted God. The crisis came at the height of our hunger strike when I was so weak I thought I'd be rushed to a hospital. It was in the dead of night, the pain was very intense, and I felt I was slipping into unconsciousness. Only then did I come to trust God absolutely and to find the courage to say, "It's all up to you now. Your will be done." Of course the struggle remains to keep that trust alive, and I know it will never be easy!

Somehow, though, with a greater trust in God's goodness and

love we become more at home in whatever situation we find ourselves, no matter how hard the circumstances. It is true, as Merton says, that "the only thing that matters is the fact of the sacrifice, the essential dedication of one's self, one's will." Doesn't this make you recall what we heard so often from those impressive basic Christian community leaders?

Liberating Spirituality

Only a liberating spirituality is relevant for us Christians today. We have no choice but to reject the kind of spirituality that has alienated us from the historical events that are part of salvation history and isolated us from the people for whom Christ made the supreme sacrifice. Today our spirituality can only blossom if we allow the Spirit to move us beyond our fears and doubts, our hesitations and insecurities. We have to believe in the power of the Spirit to push us toward new frontiers of involvement in terms of a militant gospel. The amazing grace which is God's gift of courage and justice can only be ours if we embrace the spirituality of Jesus.

In Luke 4:18-19 we see the basis of this spirituality which comes with the anointing of the Spirit. We have to be instruments by which the good news is confirmed in the lives of the poor. We have to let go of all the trimmings of a consumerist and materialistic society and take on a way of life that nurtures true human values. We have to seek the end of all forms of bondage and enslavement so that there are no more captives. Like the proverbial bird in flight, our spirituality must be founded on freedom as we seek to remain free despite threats and harassment from the powers-that-be. We must be involved in a constant dialectic with our surroundings to avoid bigotry, ignorance, shortsightedness, and superstition. It is our faith that will enable us to see the truth behind the lies and the light behind the dark curtain of despair and hopelessness. With the courage of our convictions—and for us Christians it is a faith-imperative—we are inspired to be part of the struggle that would set the oppressed free.

Our spirituality must be Christ-centered and nourished by the Spirit, who places us at the service of the poor and oppressed. This service becomes a source of grace for it facilitates the building of community among the dehumanized. Strengthened by kinship within these communities, the poor are enabled to confront the reality of social sin which evokes in them a desire to effect reconciliation. For such a reconciliation to be genuine it has to go beyond the personal level to the level of structure. The evil that lurks in the heart of the societal structure must be demolished and in its place must be established the grace that makes possible the reign of justice and peace. In the establishment of such a just and humane society the kingdom is foreshadowed. Here is made manifest the covenant of the people with the Lord of history. Class struggle would be no more since the believers would be "one in mind and heart and they would share with one another everything they have" (Acts 4:32). In such a scenario Christ reigns and our spirituality finds its fulfillment.

THE CHALLENGE TO HOPE

Some more detainees were padlocked in the jail and their bodies bore the scars of torture.

The anger I felt at this appalling display of naked, brutal force was exacerbated by the lies of "professional witnesses" used against us by the military authorities. Meanwhile, a few other detainees went through depression, and I felt helpless at being unable to offer a comforting hand.

We can only thank God that when such a moment occurs in the wake of tragedy, we still retain the embers of hope. We find hope, but not without the agony of God's seeming abandonment. It is the discovery that God is present in these moments that restores our full trust in God as our protector and defender. Anchored in the faith that we are always in God's care, and that God saves us from our enemies, our hope in the Lord takes on the characteristics of fire. It tears apart the bleak darkness of hopelessness, warms the battered heart, and raises to the heavens the prayer for strength and courage.

The amazing grace of the spirit pierces through the things that happen here in prison, and one is blessed with hope. The political detainees sing their songs, and as the music echoes through our cells, the hope that the songs bring is very palpable. These are songs about birds with freedom to fly across the heavens, about mothers bequeathing to their children the legacy of heroism, and about peasants offering their lives so that justice will reign. They also sing of hope as in the words of this song composed by a young mother, a codetainee:

> in the face of freedom caught in chains
> and the harsh brutality we encounter,
> the burden of the heart is heavy.
> but we should continue to struggle,
> no matter how painful is our suffering.
> we should never lose hope.

We are not without a source of hope from the outside. Beyond our national boundaries, friends in solidarity encourage us to take heart. And, most important, our fellow Filipinos, the millions who have come out in the open to express their outrage against the U.S.-Marcos dictatorship, have expressed their option for justice. Among other things, their voices urgently demand: FREE ALL POLITICAL PRISONERS!

To capture the mood of a people on the march to liberation, a poet-friend wrote:

> The killing of our people will stop.
> The starving of our children will end.
> We will break through our prisons
> to fight for our right to self-determination.
> Justice will prevail.
> Freedom will be ours.
> And reigning in the land
> one day will be peace.
> And only PEACE.

The belief that the Lord of history will bring us deliverance and lead us to our own promised land has made life in prison a prayer of hope in itself.

8

The Course of Justice

A political detainee is the mirror of the Filipino today.
Caught in the prison built by those who want to perpetuate
themselves in power, the detainee agonizes through the pain,
seething in anger, feeling helpless and powerless at times, but,
ultimately, always struggling to keep dignity intact despite the
odds.

K. Gaspar

MAY 26, 1983

I have been transferred from a detention center in the country's
capital to one here in the south, my hometown. It is a very welcome
change. I was kept in "isolated status" in Manila, while here I am
among close to sixty other political prisoners. I have been formally
charged with "inciting to rebellion." The evidence held against me
is that I had traveled to other countries where I supposedly con-
tacted communists to fund the underground movement. If they
only knew what happened in our theological conference in Geneva!

. . . Those of us charged with "national security crimes" are
covered under a Presidential Commitment Order (PCO), which
will not allow our release, even on bail, unless authorized by
President Marcos himself.

156

JUNE 8, 1983

The day after tomorrow I will appear before the regional trial court here in Davao City. The case may drag on for months. Witnesses of the military have a habit of not appearing at trial hearings, the result being endless postponements. Delaying justice is another form of victimization.

JULY 30, 1983

In the last four months I have been through three prisons. First they took me to Manila, then transferred me to Davao, where I was detained in the military stockade. Last July 20, at the height of a hunger strike, two of us—the German Lutheran pastor, Volker, and I—were transferred to the Davao City jail, which is a prison for convicted and suspected criminals. Our separation from the rest was a form of harassment as they suspected that we were the leaders behind the hunger strike.

SEPTEMBER 8, 1983

In today's paper Cardinal Sin is quoted as urging the government to free all political detainees. He says that their release "would heal many wounds and hasten the process of reconciliation."

. . . I am supposed to have a hearing this week but my counsel suspects another postponement. The judiciary machine runs slowly. My last hearing was two months ago.

Meanwhile, I look through the bars and see the green hills, the tall grass, and the water lilies. At night there are the stars to remind me that, despite the stark darkness, there are a million dreams to live for.

MAY 8, 1984

During all this waiting an imagery has surfaced. It is of being shipwrecked and alone on an isolated island waiting for rescue. A sailing ship passes by and brings hope of approaching help, only to drift away. After a while another boat comes into view; it looks as if this boat is really coming to rescue me. But it also disappears into the horizon.

There have been two or three occasions when my family and I thought I was on the threshold of freedom. The last one was the possibility of provisional release on bail. Friends in Manila and here in Davao had approached the authorities responsible for these decisions. There has as yet been no definite word from Manila, favorable or unfavorable, regarding our request. Apparently the opposition of the local military has been emphatic. It lost face when my case became a *cause celebre*, further exacerbated by the international brouhaha that came with the upsurge of solidarity support.

Even after a year since my disappearance the embarrassment the military suffered from my testimony in the supreme court remains unhealed. It is unfortunate that within our culture saving face takes precedence over doing what is right and just.

Right now the military is relying on the court and the legal proceedings and has adopted a hands-off policy concerning extra-legal efforts to get me released. So it looks as if we'll have to concentrate on the outcome of the case in court. As it stands, there is reason to be optimistic—there is that word again!—that the case could be dismissed on the grounds of insufficient evidence. The motion to have it dismissed is now in court, and we will hear the judge's verdict on April 17, Tuesday of Holy Week. If his verdict is negative it will not be difficult to reflect on Holy Week. Who knows, there may be another reason to celebrate Easter if "God's hour" is for me that week.

The hearing was again postponed.

JULY 9, 1984

Even if my case is dismissed, my release is not guaranteed. There are close to ten detainees here who would already have been released as their cases have been dismissed in court, but they are covered by a PCO and will only be set free if the PCO is lifted by the dictator himself. In the case of Miro, Oca, and Jong-jong, it has meant waiting since last August! The utter injustice of it all—

languishing in jail without any case against them. There is word now that they may soon be released. We can only hope they will be out of here soon, for they have waited too long.

AUGUST 13, 1984

There is a breakthrough in the legal proceedings regarding my case. At my hearing last July 23, my lawyers requested the court for a marathon hearing, from August 15 through 17, for the presentation of my defense. The military's "professional witnesses" have claimed that I did acts tantamount to inciting people to rebellion, and those are the claims that have to be refuted.

THE CHARGES AGAINST KARL

In the presentation of their case against Karl, the combined military-civilian team of prosecution lawyers brought forth witnesses who testified that on certain dates in 1980 and 1981 Karl was giving seminars and lectures to rebel groups in certain provinces of the Philippines.

Charge: April 1980—Karl visited a "red zone" and incited the people to join the revolution.
Defense: During this time Karl was responsible for a Mindanao-Sulu pastoral conference. Two bishops were among those who gave evidence.

Charge: Oct. 1980—Same charge as above.
Defense: Karl was in Mexico and Central America.

Charge: Nov. 1980—He attended a meeting of top communist leaders.
Defense: He was in Chile, Argentina, and Brazil.

Charge: Feb. 1981—He lectured to communist cadres in the south of the Philippines.
Defense: He was working with the National Secretariat for Social Action in Manila while preparing his papers for Australia.

Charge: Aug. 1981—He attended a top meeting of communist cadres.

Defense: He was in the United States at the invitation of the Maryknoll Fathers.

AUGUST 13, 1984

In relation to the government's charges against me, there is no question but that I am innocent. If there is any justice in our judiciary system I will, of course, be acquitted as my defense can easily prove my innocence. But who can trust our courts these days? But for a few exceptions most of our judges from the supreme court down to the municipal courts have not found the courage to stand independent of the dictatorship.

Given this precarious situation we can't rule out the possibility of conviction. Mine is literally a showcase, and the military top brass are hoping, and maybe pressuring the courts, that I be convicted. They have been banking on their "strong evidence" against me so that I'll be found guilty, if only to save face since, supposedly, I have brought them a lot of embarrassment. They fired the former judge advocate because most of those brought to trial were acquitted or their cases were dismissed for lack of evidence. In an area like Davao, which is considered a "war zone," the top military echelon here naturally want to see all political detainees convicted. They are under pressure "to deliver," and their performance is measured by how many alleged CPP-NPA subversives they can present to their commander-in-chief, who would like to see all alleged subversives jailed for life or sentenced to death. This is now the penalty, as stated in Presidential Decree 1834, for those found guilty of subversion and rebellion.

There are about a dozen detainees here who would already have been released if it were not for their PCO and the subsequent red tape. The most frustrating case, however, is that of the Skyline Group (Fr. Dong Tizon, Amy, Nat, Virgie, and Betty, who were arrested almost two years ago). Everything that could go wrong happened in the course of their legal proceedings. First, there were so many postponed scheduled hearings. Then, after a year, the judge retired so there had to be a raffle to have another judge assigned to the case. Meanwhile the court stenographer hadn't finished transcribing his notes, and now, having left his job, he was nowhere to be found. A second judge was assigned to the case but after one hearing the fiscal moved to remove him because of "fraternity connections" with the husband of one of the accused. They now have to look for another judge and find ways of securing the stenographer's notes. The group is about to "celebrate" a second anniversary in prison!

THE HEARING, AUGUST 15-17

During the hearing Bishop Escaler, who was called to witness to Karl's presence at the Mindanao-Sulu Pastoral Conference in April 1980, spoke of the letter of thanks signed by three archbishops and eleven bishops of Mindanao-Sulu which was given to Karl during that conference. Entitled "Testimony of Gratitude to Karl Gaspar," the letter stated: "We would like to acknowledge publicly your invaluable services and extraordinary dedicated example as a Catholic layman and administrator towards the building up of our Christian communities in Mindanao-Sulu." In particular, the fourteen members of the MSPC hierarchy cited Karl's "great generosity of soul, zeal for God's kingdom, patience and charity in the midst of difficulties, and the sacrifice of your time, abilities, and yourself without regard for personal convenience."

When asked his reaction to Karl's arrest and the subsequent accusations by the military, Bishop Escaler spoke in a loud and clear voice: "I was shocked; I was angry. . . . Whatever was said by the military agents against this man was lies." He also said that "all my complaints about these charges against Karl fell on deaf ears because of their [the officials'] concern for national security. . . . I appealed to the president, to the military, to everyone I knew in high office—all to no avail." Later, when asked about this statement outside the court, the bishop said, "I wanted to state in the strongest possible words my condemnation of what the military was trying to do. It was diabolical!"

Karl was questioned in court about some subversive materials and ammunitions that the military "found" when they raided his office some time after his arrest. Karl said, "These items are not known to me." His attorney noted that the list of items made out by the military was dated the day before the raid ever took place!

AUGUST 17, 1984

Finally it's over. I would like to thank you all for remembering me on those days of the marathon hearings. The prayers made possible the small miracles. Thanks especially to those who came to the hearings. Your presence provided not only the needed moral support, but also served as witness to my innocence.

The whole experience was extremely interesting. Mark 13:9-13 became real and I felt very privileged to have been a part of an experience that in a small way fulfilled the scriptures: "They will hand you over to the courts."

> When men take you off into custody,
> do not worry beforehand about
> what to say. In that hour, say
> what you are inspired to say. It
> will not be yourselves speaking
> but the Holy Spirit [Mark 13:11].

We were in the court not really to prove that I was innocent of the charges filed by the regime against me, but to preach the good news and to bear witness to the truth embodied in the gospel.

The bulk of the testimonies was meant to discredit the affidavits and court testimonies of the military's professional witnesses. We wanted to show that they had committed perjury. So those who took the stand in my defense testified to my having been with them on the crucial dates in April, October, and November 1980 as well as February 5 and August 6-8 in 1981. While my witnesses' main function was to present the necessary alibis, it was inevitable that they would touch on matters related to the situation—the church's involvement in justice and human rights issues, the law and the gospel, and the imperative option that Christians must make in defense of human dignity. The witnesses found it easy to testify because they were asked to tell the truth and "nothing but the truth." Within the circumstances of the case, it was inevitable that the witness stand became a pulpit. We took turns in giving sermons. Poor judge—he must have found it disconcerting!

Toward the end of the marathon I took the stand. Among the

things that I had to speak about were: the circumstances of my arrest, how my rights were violated, where I was during the crucial dates, my work at MSPC, what I did during my trips abroad in 1980 and 1981, why I have become a human rights advocate, the underlying reasons for my commitment to justice, and my opinion on the relevant topics—martial law, violence or nonviolence as a strategy for change, the fairness of our courts, and the need for reform in government. I was well prepared and the presence of family and friends, the solid testimony of my witnesses, and the encouragement of my fellow detainees contributed to my high moral.

The judge has a maximum of ninety days to give his decision although the custom is to give it within thirty days. Will I be acquitted or not? We can only wait and see!

Shalom,

Karl

9

Epilogue:
A Letter from Jim Wallis

October 25, 1984

My dear brother Karl,

Lately I've been rereading your letters and reflections from prison. They have become spiritual reading for me. Your epistles have served to strengthen my faith and make me confident in hope. And I know I'm not the only one. In the mystery and grace of God, your imprisonment has touched the lives and strengthened the hearts of God's people laboring for justice and for peace all over this world.

The government thought they could silence your voice and curtail your activity by throwing you in prison; instead your witness is clearer, and you have inspired many others to action. Karl, your imprisonment has indeed furthered the cause of the gospel and rebounded to the glory of God.

I cannot help but recall the words of Paul written from a jail cell where he also suffered as a political prisoner. It seems to me now that these words apply to your own imprisonment:

> I want you to know, brethren, that what has happened to me has really served to advance the gospel, so that it has become known throughout the whole praetorian guard and to all the

rest that my imprisonment is for Christ; and most of the brethren have been made confident in the Lord because of my imprisonment, and are much more bold to speak the word of God without fear [Phil. 1:12–14].

They have locked up your body, but they have not imprisoned your spirit. They have taken away your liberty, but you are still free. They have controlled your movements, but they haven't controlled your conscience. They have accused you with lies, but they have not been able to suppress the truth. They have tried to silence you, but your voice is stronger than ever. They have taken you from your community, but you have formed another one behind the bars. They have tried to quench your faith, but the fires of persecution have only made it stronger.

My brother, you are not alone in that jail cell. The grace of God is clearly with you as are the love and prayers of countless Christians in the Philippines and around the world, many of whom you will never know but who are united with you in the bonds of Christian fellowship.

As for me, my love and friendship for you have grown stronger and stronger over these many months, and I feel even closer to you than before your ordeal began. Keeping you in my thoughts and prayers has been a great blessing to me. It has been an occasion of true joy, the kind that comes mingled with sadness and tears.

I rejoice in you, my friend and brother. I rejoice in your faith and in your hope. And I rejoice in the Lord, who has made us one.

Love and Solidarity,

Jim

Abbreviations and Acronyms

AI	Amnesty International
AMRSP	Association of Major Religious Superiors of the Philippines
APHD	Asian Partners for Human Development
ASI	Asian Social Institute
AWD	Action for World Development
BCC	Basic Christian Community
BMA	Bangsa Moro Army (the military arm of the MNLF)
CBCP	Catholic Bishops' Conference of the Philippines
CEBEMO	Dutch bishops' funding agency
CHDF	Civil Home Defense Force
CO	commanding officer
CPP	Communist Party of the Philippines
FLAG	Free Legal Assistance Group
HCCD	Holy Cross College of Digos (Davao del Sur)

IBP	Integrated Bar of the Philippines
IMF–WB	International Monetary Fund–World Bank
JAJA	Justice for Aquino, Justice for All movement
Lakbayan	see glossary
MetroDisCom	Metropolitan District Command
MIA	Manila International Airport
MIG	Military Intelligence Group
MNLF	Moro National Liberation Front
MSPC	Mindanao-Sulu Pastoral Conference
NDF	National Democratic Front
NPA	New Peoples' Army
PAASCU	Private Association for the Accreditation of Colleges and Universities
PC	Philippine Constabulary
PC/INP	Philippine Constabulary/Integrated National Police
PCO	Presidential Commitment Order
PDA	Preventive Detention Action
PDO	Poor, Deprived, and Oppressed
PLM	Philippine Liberation Movement
PNA	Philippine Nurses Association

R.G.S.	Religious of the Good Shepherd
R2	Military Intelligence Unit
SocDem	Social Democrats
TFDP	Task Force for Detainees Philippines
TNC	Transnational corporation
TROCAIRE	A Gaelic word meaning mercy; it is the name of the Irish bishops' agency for Third World development
UCCP	United Church of Christ of the Philippines
WATCH	Women's Association for True Change

Glossary

alalay	Tagalog slang meaning a buddy who can be relied upon
anawim	a Hebrew word meaning "the poor" or "the little ones"
barkada	a group (particularly a group of young persons) who stick together
bartolina	a very small, dark, unventilated room for solitary confinement
buryong	a Davao word suggesting a drastic manifestation of patience running out, coupled with a series of feelings of ennui, anger, and helplessness
desaparecidos	those who have disappeared
First Quarter Storm	a reference to encounters between the military and the students in premartial law days, during which some students were killed
hulbot	a Cebuano word meaning "to abduct," usually in order to kill
kinilaw	a dish, usually of raw fish, prepared with vinegar and spices

kuya	appellation for an elder brother or for one who is like an elder brother
Lakbayan	*Lakad ng Bayan para sa Kalayaan* (people's walk for freedom)
laya	a Tagalog word meaning "freedom"
Mabini lawyers	a group of lawyers who offer services to political detainees
malong	name of the *sarong* worn by the Muslims
narra	mahogany
niños	infants or small children
Pasyon	life and death of Jesus Christ in vernacular verse, chanted for a whole day and night without pausing during the Lenten Week
poblacion	a town proper
polar bear	a Chinese all-purpose (menthol) medicine
puhon	a Visayan word meaning "God willing"
Ramadhan	the Muslim month of fasting. *Duyog Ramadhan* refers to a Christian movement in Mindanao of solidarity with the Muslims in their fast
safehouse	a term used to designate a place which is under the jurisdiction of military intelligence units and to which political detainees are taken, usually blindfolded, and where various forms of maltreatment and torture are administered to them

salvaging   extrajudicial and summary execution

SocDem   Social Democrat

strategic hamlet   forced evacuation centers

Tandang Sora   a Filipina heroine

Trocaire   see Abbreviations and Acronyms

Karl is now free but more than *one thousand* political detainees remain imprisoned in jails and military camps throughout the Philippines.

If you would like to protest this violation of human rights, please write your protest to:

President Ferdinand Marcos
Malacanang Palace
Manila, Philippines

or

Minister Juan Ponce Enrile
Ministry of National Defense
Camp Aguinaldo, Quezon City
Philippines

If you would like to know more information about the Philippine situation or about the political detainees in particular, please write to:

Task Force for Detainees Philippines
214 N. Domingo
Quezon City, Philippines